SIGN
POSTS

EARL PALMER

SIGN POSTS

*Living with Christian Values
in an Age of Uncertainty*

WORD PUBLISHING
Dallas · London · Sydney · Singapore

SIGNPOSTS

Library of Congress Cataloging-in-Publication Data

Palmer, Earl F.
    Signposts / Earl F. Palmer.
        p.   cm.
    Includes bibliographical references.
    ISBN 0-8499-3223-8
    1. Christian life—1960–   2. Conduct of life.   3. Values.
I. Title.
BV4501.2.P275   1990
248.4—dc20   89–48074
                                               CIP

0 1 2 3 9 RRD 9 8 7 6 5 4 3 2 1

Printed in the United States of America

For PETE and ERIC,
WUMAO and WESLEY

and

the students in my life

Remembering my friends who I loved in the
simpler times of youth will help me
be a friend.
Remembering the songs and the shows that they go with
makes new songs easier to learn.
Remembering my home as the place always for me
makes me more at home when I am away.
Remembering my name and the dreams I made
my own
gives me strength when people wonder who I am.
Remembering the love that found me before I could
remember
keeps life alive while I am remembering.

E.F.P.

Contents

Preface:
"All the Difference"

I carve inscriptions on pieces of driftwood each summer, and my family and friends sometimes make requests of me which I try to fulfill. Last summer I had a request for a line from a Robert Frost poem. Frost tells his readers in the poem that he chose "a road less travelled" and that as he looked back upon that choice he realized that his choice on that late afternoon "has made all the difference." I carved the words "And that has made all the difference."

At the same time I was carving I was also at work on this book about biblical wisdom and the search for values. I discovered that wisdom in the Bible is understood as a skill at finding the true pathway in the places where there are many pathways to choose from; and I discovered, not only in the Bible, but also from my own life and living, that the choices make a profound difference.

This book is a study of wisdom in its Old Testament and New Testament settings, and it is a study of some of the major signposts that point the way for today's sojourners. Such a study inevitably becomes a study of the theology of the sojourner, and I hope that these pages will help all sojourners in their choices of pathways that deserve the journey and in the journey itself.

I owe my thanks for the people of my own journeying, and I want to express that gratitude. To my parents, my wife Shirley, and our three children, Anne, Jon and Elizabeth, our borrowed sons Pete Balaam and Eric Jacobson, and two Mount Shasta friends, Wumao Ye and Wesley Zhang.

So many people helped me, too: my secretary Patti Nicolson, my typist Mary Phillips, my colleagues in ministry and members of First Presbyterian Church of Berkeley. Finally a special thanks to the teachers and students at the Trinity Theological College, Singapore, and the English Language Teachers to China Conference in Hong Kong who first heard these thoughts on finding our way.

Earl Palmer
Berkeley, California

Introduction:
Values

What is a human value? Here is one definition that makes sense to me: *A value is a personal conviction about living which means so much to me that I have come to treasure it and I intend to hold on to it throughout my life.* My values are convictions that I am not about either to give up or give up on. As do all men and women, I have values. In one way or another every day I make a whole range of decisions about the events and experiences of that day which are determined by the values I hold. In the same way my daily decisions, in a thousand ways, change and refine, deepen or diminish the values that I hold and treasure.

The Bible is a Book of values just as any book I read or write is a book of values. Even my checkbook and the datebook I keep document the values of my life because they tell stories about my own daily priorities and goals, my responsibilities and dreams for the future.

Where do we find durable and worthwhile values? The Book of Proverbs challenges us to make wisdom our first value. I am convinced from my own experiences that the advice found there is very wise, a little like an Alpine guide who, before the expedition actually is under way, first teaches a group of climbers the skills of reading a map and the ways of rope technique and snow survival. The climbers will require this wisdom before they need courage or stamina. And without Alpine wisdom they will be downright dangerous to each other and themselves.

There arrives an early-in-the-morning moment on some definite day when the expedition must begin its climb. On that day the skills will be joined together with such other values as determination, loyalty, integrity, courage, etc. The result of the trek will depend upon the total mixture of values and the degree of personal commitment to those values that each climber has within himself or herself.

Ordinary daily life is similar to my Alpine adventure. Each of us must explore the values that we choose to bring to that daily journey. I have already named wisdom as the first value, but there are more that follow. The Old Testament presents many values. We find them in the Law and the Prophets, the Proverbs and the Songs, in the promises of the Old Testament. The New Testament is also a book of values, whether they are found in the Gospels or the Letters of Paul and John, Peter and James. In this book it is my goal to explore ten of those values that have their origin in the Old and New Testaments. These values are very old and yet, because they still work well in daily pathfinding, they have the advantages of authenticity and trustworthiness to commend them.

A value is not truthful and good simply because it is old. Many false values are very old and, therefore, tradition alone can never be a sufficient validation of a reason or goal for my life. Human history has proven that many traditions are not verifiable by this threefold test: Is the value faithful to God's self-disclosure of his will for our lives? Is the value experientially useful? and has the value endured the test of time? It is true that there are values which are handed down from one generation to the next. For that reason, we are at first tempted to overrate the importance of such a value simply because of its longevity. But its durability may not be a sign of its truthfulness.

The hostility between the two Italian families of Montague and Capulet in Shakespeare's *Romeo and Juliet* was a very old feud. It had the full endorsement of tradition to validate its intense hatred. In a certain odd and perverse way the feud even worked well experientially and gave purpose to the young hotheads in each family. But in Shakespeare's story the tradition is a bad one. Romeo of the house of Montague and Juliet of the house of Capulet were right to challenge it. The hatred was old and durable and each side had a catalogue of complaints to justify the animosity. Nevertheless, the tradition was not wise because it failed on two counts. Its anger went contrary to the good will of God for each family and secondly the practical experiential effect of the feud was finally destructive, counterproductive, and had altogether bad results in the lives of those who slavishly followed the tradition. It helped the youth to fight and its result was death and despair.

From this one example we can see how important it is to think carefully about the values by which we propose to live our lives. We need to continually test every motivation and every value through the wisdom lens of the threefold test: Is it righteous? Is it worthy? Will it last? This book deals with values and looks at some of the ways we test their validity and the ways that they test ours.

-1-
Five Ways of
Finding Ourselves

Have you ever been lost on some trip or journey? Somehow while you are en route that sudden awareness hits you that you don't really know where you are. I have been thinking about some of the problems and the ways of getting lost. From my own experience, there are five main ways that this can happen. For example, I get lost when I cannot understand what the street signs say. It is a little like being in an evergreen forest with a slip of paper that gives very precise directions telling me to be sure to turn right when the medium-sized Douglas fir appears alongside the trail. But what if the hiker is a commodity trader from downtown Chicago who thinks all evergreens are alike? The directions are true, the signs are in place, but the hiker is still lost. Ask him about exchange rates and certificates of deposit as directional markers, and he will find the way. Ask about a Douglas fir, however, and he is lost.

I have experienced another kind of lostness on several occasions in mountain treks. A bank of fog comes in upon the places where I am trying to make key directional decisions. The signs are present and I would be able to understand them if I could only *see* them. I am lost in a place where on a clear day I would easily find my way.

A third kind of lostness happens when I forget the directions that were given to me. Jill and Eustace have this problem in C. S. Lewis's *Silver Chair* when they forget at key moments the four signs that Aslan the great golden Lion had told them to remember for their journey.

A fourth kind of lostness is interpersonal, and it happens when somehow I am separated from the people in my life. Though I may know where I am, I am still lost from those I need and want to be near. The street scene at the opening of the film, *Empire of the Sun*, portrays a violent kind of lostness. The English boy is separated from his mother and father during the panic in the streets of Shanghai during the Japanese attack upon that city in the early days of World War II.

There is a fifth kind of lostness that is the most dangerous of all, because it involves a deliberate and wrongful deciding or nondeciding of my own mind and heart. This is the lostness that happens when I deliberately disregard clear and understandable signposts and set out in a direction that does not carry me where I really want to go or should go.

An Embarrassing Experience

This reminds me of an embarrassing journeying experience of my own. When I was a student at Princeton Seminary I and my California friends made regular trips by car across America from California to Princeton. We drove the 3,000 miles nonstop and did so by rotating the driving. On one such trip there were three of us: Donn Moomaw, Dick Jacobson, and myself in the car and we were traveling to California for the summer break. On what was to become an unforgettable night in that journey, Donn was the driver. He came into a small town somewhere in Iowa; it was about 1:30 A.M. and only one gas station was open. He made a U-turn to pull into the station and then awakened me for my turn to drive. He then promptly went to sleep in the back seat. I paid for the gas and began my driving assignment unaware of the U-turn into the station. Without realizing it, I was headed back toward the East Coast! I actually drove for some three hours in that direction which made matters all the worse. Two humorous incidents did occur during that drive. A Greyhound bus came toward me and on its front was emblazoned the city name, *Denver.* I remember thinking to myself how careless of that driver to have the wrong city name on the front of his bus. It should have said *Chicago*, I thought to myself. A second bus with the name *Salt Lake City* passed me. Again I chuckled to myself. "What is that company coming to with such incompetence among its maintenance people?" Then I saw the ribbon of light of the morning sun coming up over the horizon and at that point I made an abrupt U-turn without waking my passengers. A little later, however, when we were all about to stop for breakfast, Donn was sure he had seen these towns before. At that point I admitted to my fellow travelers the unfortunate though understandable mistake that I had made.

I remember we had two discussions. One was a mathematical one as we tried to calculate the time we had lost—was it three hours, six hours, nine hours or even twelve hours? Then, there was the ethical question of who should pay for the gasoline for this misdirectioned mishap. Ironically, of course, the town markers of Iowa meant little to me. However, the Denver and Salt Lake City signs should have. I should have obeyed those signs or at least consulted our map. Finally, the sun did it for me. Isaiah 9:2 would always mean a lot more to me from this point on in my life. "The people who walked in darkness have seen a great light."

Each of these forms of lostness can happen to any of us in a concrete geographical sense, but they also may have more than time and geographic importance. They have moral, intellectual, and spiritual significance as well.

Forms of Lostness

It is possible to become ideologically and psychologically lost because we cannot locate any distinctive historical markers alongside the pathway of our life journeys. We may become, in effect, nonhistorical people who have little or no awareness of these distinctive markers that make up the landscape contours of our own unique identity. This is the cultural, historical drift about which Allan Bloom warns us in his book, *The Closing of the American Mind*. We all know people who aren't aware of the great classic sources of their own Western civilization. What of those who have no real awareness of the great biblical sources too? People can become so present-existence-oriented that they have a very fragile sense of their own past history—or of the history of civilization itself. They become self-referential, lacking outer reference points. Victor Hugo describes the firebrand revolutionary leader Enjolras in this way. "He had passion for revolution but little passion or knowledge for civilization."

Consider also the lostness of confusion in which a blurring occurs that distorts our vision and our ability to think clearly. Chemical additives like drugs and alcohol are very common ways in which we actually self-produce a fog layer around our lives so that we cannot think or see clearly or wisely. There are other fogs too; there may be emotional confusion that has its origin in hurtful and unresolved experiences in my life with the result that there is a blurring of what I see. These hurtful experiences become like alien criteria that influence my perception even though they should not have the influence that they have. An abusive home experience in childhood now blurs the vision in young adulthood.

All misdirections have one thing in common; they happen in very small degrees at first. I may have taken very small missteps and moved toward a lostness which only later on becomes evident and obvious. In the same way, I usually forget things in small and nonobvious ways until they finally gather together to become a major missing piece in the puzzle of my life. In my youth I may set out on a "disconnection-from-people" lifestyle. Thus I enter my young adult years with an obvious isolation in which I am lonely and separated from people I really wanted to know. It may begin early in my life with hardly noticeable effects, but it really hurts in the young adult years.

What are the cures for these experiences of losing our way? Just as the five kinds of lostness I have described reach their most painful level in the young adult years, at the same time I believe it is during these same years that effective help can be brought into our lives. This help can have the most creative and healing effect. I believe this is one reason why the years of youth are so vitally important. During the late teens and early twenties, young people are able to make major redirection decisions because the willingness to risk has not yet been replaced with those obstinate refusal defenses which are a roadblock to growth in the adult who no longer feels young enough to make major changes. This possibility for change is what makes the young adult years so vitally important in the character development of a person.

The solutions for lostness are usually not immediate because redirection is a step-by-step process. It is an incremental finding of the right pathway. The finding begins with signposts that we discover, and the Bible is the place I want to begin our search. We are looking for markers that we can read and really understand.

If the "lost" experience is incremental and gradual, so also is the experience of finding our way. At least for most people, a gradual and incremental gathering up of evidence and directional markers is their experience. Little by little, we discover where we really are and where we really want to go. What happens is that we decide to look for markers and to learn how to read them. We discover that there are no advantages to ignorance. When we in Western culture began to lose the great markers of the Bible as a working part of our life we found ourselves not only without the Ten Commandments Law to make us feel guilty but also without the gospel to give us hope. The result is the formless landscape of which T. S. Eliot warned us when he criticized the hero/heroine in the modern novel: "The modern hero does not have a conscience, only nervous reactions." Without the struggle with conscience we become our own reference points and this is why such novels as Eliot has in mind lack that quality of consequence that in the end creates real drama. This is because it takes substance in a character in a novel or play to give to a story a sense of total consequence, and substance comes from that character who comes up against the demands and hopes of culture, of conscience, of the Law and of the gospel.

We need markers for our lives just as we need people in our lives. Are we lost because we have lost touch with other people? We need to cut through the fog of every alien imposition upon our life journey, whether it is chemical or psychological, and we need to remember the markers that we have found. All this takes time and a certain skill. Let us think first of all about the skill.

-2-
Wisdom

Wisdom is the very first signpost to watch for, yet wisdom is not so much a signpost as it is the ability to *see* the signposts. It is not so much a great value (like truth and love and courage) as it is a way of *finding* values like these. The word "wisdom" and its equivalent in each language system has won the respect of every generation and every culture though its meanings vary.

The ancient Greeks treasured wisdom (Sophia), and their love (philia) of wisdom has given Western language one of our most honored words: *philosophy*. Aristotle understood wisdom as a profound inner attachment to the true good. For him, therefore, wisdom was primarily ideological.

In Asia, Confucianist thought defines wisdom as the respect of a man or woman for the knowledge of previous generations. Thus, for Confucius, wisdom was primarily personal and relational.

The Hebrew language has a very concrete word for wisdom, and it is the word *Hakam* which means "skill." Even more precisely, it is the skill learned from three sources: from God, from my own experiences of testing various kinds of wisdom over time, and from people in my life who are my teachers in the way of wisdom. The New Testament is written in Greek, but its writers think in the Hebrew meanings. Thus, this Old Testament

Hakam wisdom is the underpinning foundation for the New Testament teaching about the role of wisdom in our lives. It is both ideological and personal. Notice how the three sources for the skill called wisdom each converge in the Book of Proverbs:

The Proverbs of Solomon, Son of David, king of Israel:

> That men may know wisdom and instruction,
>   understand words of insight,
> receive instruction in wise dealing,
>   righteousness, justice, and equity;
> that prudence may be given to the simple,
>   knowledge and discretion to the youth—
> the wise man also may hear and increase in learning,
>   And the man of understanding acquire skill,
> to understand a proverb and a figure,
>   the words of the wise and their riddles.
> The fear of the Lord is the beginning of knowledge;
>   fools despise wisdom and instruction.
> Hear, my son, your father's instruction,
>   and reject not your mother's teaching;
> for they are a fair garland for your head,
>   and pendants for your neck.

Notice the emphasis upon the skill of wisdom and its dynamic nature as a growing skill. But the skill begins with the discovery of God. And that discovery is endorsed to us by good people in our lives, such as our mothers and fathers. What now follows these general principles is a story in which wisdom is severely tempted:

> My son, if sinners entice you,
>   do not consent.

If they say, "Come with us, let us lie in wait for blood,
>   let us wantonly ambush the innocent;
like Sheol let us swallow them alive
>   and whole, like those who go down to the Pit;
we shall find all precious goods,
>   we shall fill our houses with spoil;
throw in your lot among us,
>   we will all have one purse"—
my son, do not walk in the way with them,
>   hold back your foot from their paths;
for their feet run to evil,
>   and they make haste to shed blood.
For in vain is a net spread
>   in the sight of any bird;
but these men lie in wait for their own blood,
>   they set an ambush for their own lives.
Such are the ways of all who get gain by violence;
>   it takes away the life of its possessors.

The story about the treachery of the bad friends is followed with the words of that insight that can only result from a look at life from a long term vantage point.

Wisdom cries aloud in the street;
>   in the markets she raises her voice;
on the top of the walls she cries out;
>   at the entrance of the city gates she speaks;
"How long, O simple ones, will you love being simple?
How long will scoffers delight in their scoffing
>   and fools hate knowledge?
Give heed to my reproof;
behold I will pour out my thoughts to you."

(Proverbs 1:1–23)

Finally the writer of the Proverbs speaks the promises and the warnings together in order to call each of us to discover wisdom. According to this first chapter of Proverbs the three-sourced skill called wisdom is the ability I need to find the right path for my life journey and then to stay on it. It is a skill that cuts through various kinds of moral and intellectual fog, because it recognizes the blur of false criteria when the blurring is happening. This wisdom and skill is always learning how to stay in touch with the people who travel alongside, and it even defeats the forgetfulness that becomes one opportunity for every temptation with important facts about God's character and truth remembered.

The Book of Proverbs first of all tells of the beginning of wisdom as fear or reverence toward God. It implies respectful obedience toward what God has revealed to us of his will for our lives in the Law and the Covenants that he has given. This beginning place stands throughout the Bible as the essential reference point for the skill of wisdom.

Our Reference Point

We are to begin with God's revelation as the reference point. The reference point is not ourselves or the influence of anyone around us. This beginning place is vital to the logic of the Old Testament Book of Proverbs and the New Testament Sermon on the Mount if the traveler is going to find his or her way. It is like the discovery of true North on a compass or the North Star in the evening sky. Every future direction choice will depend upon that source direction that is both prior to other directions and is faithfully true.

We have a starting point from which to encourage our journey when we are correctly set on course. Also, it is a correction point from which to find ourselves when we have moved off course. Wisdom then is a skill that both cheers us at certain directional moments in our lives and it is also a skill that rebukes us when we have made wrong choices. Wisdom plays both a positive and a negative role in our daily lives. Therefore, wisdom is always our good friend but not always the companion we choose to go with us. When we choose pathways that are false we leave the skill of wisdom behind.

The Proverb has realistically pictured for us the testing role of *Hakam*. In the Proverb a young man is tempted to disregard God's will about the violence against a neighbor and about the wrongfulness of theft. He meets certain friends who tell him of another skillfulness, another form of "wisdom" in which they as clever and proficient thieves will build an entrapment against an unsuspecting traveler so that these conspirators may become rich at the expense of their victim. The Proverb calls upon the young man, who is now tempted by his friends' proposal of a false direction, to test and examine this old and evidently foolproof proposal of robbery. He is to test the temptation first by the compass setting of God's will revealed in God's Laws against murder and robbery ("Their feet run to evil . . . . make haste to shed blood") and he is also encouraged to test the temptation pragmatically by his examination of the realistic consequences of such a lifestyle choice. "Those who set traps end up snared by the traps they set." These two tests become practical examples of the skill of wisdom in the Proverb. The young man also is encouraged to learn skills for living from his mother and his father who are mandated by the Proverb to teach the way of righteousness to their children ("Hear your father's instruction . . . your mother's teaching . . ."–v.8).

The Source of Wisdom

It is very important for us to understand this three-fold source for the skill of wisdom. We must not misunderstand that its fundamental beginning place is the revelation of God's character and will ("righteousness, justice, and equity"). We are to learn first from the Law and the gospel that comes from God himself. Our parents are another source for the skill. They teach us the ways of the skill of righteousness. However, the teaching of our parents is not portrayed as absolute in itself because their teaching is itself to be tested by the standard of God's truth. The final source is our own experience and our own necessary daily act of testing each of the alternatives by the standard of God's revealed will.

The testing is a key element in the Old and New Testament understanding of wisdom. It means we are never to see ourselves as slavishly obedient to any human influence. That even includes the influence of our parents and grandparents. If they were to advise us in the art of theft or murder, then the logic of the Proverb holds without wavering. We are to reject that advice regardless of its familial or national origin. We must reject such advice because it goes against the revealed will of God in his Law and in his promise. Such counsel, regardless of its source, is counsel toward evil. God's law must prevail even over against the advice of parents or kings if that counsel is false.

Even experiences may not be a true guide. We are now able to understand that remarkable boldness of the prophet Nathan who challenged Israel's most beloved and powerful leadership symbol—David the king. It was Nathan who said against David the popular king, "Thou art the man." Such a confrontation could only happen in a place and time where wisdom means more than obedience toward respected leaders.

Wisdom knows from experience that power and position do not automatically equal right. Might does not make right in the logic of wisdom. It is clear that a new set standard for finding the pathway is at work. It is a way of journeying in which each man and woman must weigh the influences that present themselves for our deciding. Then we must decide on the basis of the weighing of each possible way to journey in the quest of the direction what is the proper one to take on the basis of the standard of our reverence for God.

This skill for the act of deciding is what wisdom is all about. As the first chapter of Proverbs has shown us, this skill is much more complicated than simple obedience to parents or leaders, whether in the Church or the nation; wisdom is therefore one of the great freedom words of the Bible. Each of us on the journey must test the various alternatives for ourselves. And we must learn how to test each alternative. Therefore, for that person who is in the tradition of the *Hakam* wisdom of the Bible it will not be enough for us to hear the strong appeal to generational traditions—as if the opinion of previous generations were the inflexibly wise course for us to follow. Although we must honor our parents, we do not necessarily obey them in all instances. We cannot simply follow the opinion and guidance of any leader without submitting that counsel to the test of the wise and faithful will of God.

St. Paul certainly has this in mind when he reminds the Corinthians that in that moment when they followed Jesus Christ as their Lord they each chose a course direction on their individual life journeys that went counter to the wisdom of their own city, Corinth. This is what he means when he observes: "Not many of you were wise according to worldly standards . . ." (1 Corinthians 1:26). The wisdom of Corinth in the first century was exploitative and outrageously luxurious as that city had built its economy and lifestyle upon the exploitation of seagoing travelers and upon the personal wreckage of human slaves who supported the lavish luxury of Corinth. (Some first century scholars estimate that 400,000 slaves were held in bondage by the wealthy merchants of Corinth.) Had the Corinthians followed the "wisdom" skills of their city they would never have followed the gospel of 1 Corinthians 13. The quality of that love was foolishness to the cynical and prevailing consciousness of their city. But there were a few in Corinth who saw the deeper wisdom of Jesus Christ, and they chose to trust in God instead of Corinth. Therefore Paul reminds them of that choice when he says, "He is the source of your life in Christ Jesus, whom God made our wisdom, our righteousness and sanctification and redemption" (1 Corinthians 1:30).

This skill of wisdom is no easy thing, but it is very good. It is the skill of choosing the right path whether we live in Corinth or New York or Berkeley, and then staying on that pathway because of the faithful and wise companion who not only calls us to the right pathway but journeys with us. Fortunate it is for us that when we lose the way he does not.

-3-

Trust God

I remember an evening at Forest Home Christian Conference Center when several of us who were young pastors and youth workers spent an evening with the late Dr. Henrietta Mears. She was the founder of Forest Home and for many years the Director of Christian Education at the Hollywood Presbyterian Church. Dr. Mears, then in her seventies, was a mentor to each of us and we all greatly admired her personal Christian stature and leadership. One person in our group asked Miss Mears this question: "If you were going to do it all over again, is there anything you would do differently?" I remember thinking to myself as this question was being asked that the question seemed impudent and brash. Evidently Dr. Mears did not think so because without a moment of hesitation she answered the question. "I would trust God more" was her reply, and I was electrified by that wonderful response from a woman who was already a person of great faith. Of course she was right! Trust God more; that is all that she would change because that is the most basic change of all for anyone to make. If every believer did this, what changes would result!

Three Commandments for Today

It should not be surprising to us that the first three commandments of the Ten Commandments concern our trust in God. The three also dominate the New Testament.

Jesus concluded his most famous discourse, *The Sermon on the Mount,* with a parable about the wisdom of our trust in his promises and commands, "Every one then who hears these words of mine and does them will be like a wise man . . ." (Matthew 7:24). The word "hear" that Jesus uses is a great word in Hebrew: it is the word *Shema.* Every celebration of the Sacred Service since the earliest days of Jewish worship begins with that word from Deuteronomy 6. "Hear O Israel"—"Hear" means to trust and to do, to understand and to follow the will of God as revealed in his holy Law. But at the deepest level it means even more. The Bible invites us to trust God and know him, as the God of character and personhood. This invitation is profoundly more personal for us than a call to obedience before great policy statements that come from God's secretariat. Thus, when we reflect upon the opening sentences of the Ten Commandments we are hearing the language of relationship and trust more than the language of ideology and case law.

"You shall have no other gods before me" (Exodus 20:3). The Ten Commandments begin with three imperatives that have to do with our relationship to God. The first is the briefest of the three, and it makes a positive affirmation in negative terms. In this commandment we see the personal God of character set over against the false gods. The most dramatic positive fact about this commandment is its abrupt and intense personal pronoun that becomes the key linguistic center of the commandment: "No other gods before me."

The holy name for God, Yahweh, which was first introduced to Moses as the personal intransitive verb "I am," "he is," becomes the most important of all the names of God for Israel. Moses is the one who heard this self-disclosure at the burning bush: "I am who I Aм. . . . Say this to the people of Israel, 'I Aм has sent me to you'" (Exodus 3:13–15). We now meet this same personal identification of God in the first commandment. The Ten Commandments begin on this totally personal ground: the God of character exists, and therefore no other gods can compare with the One who has revealed himself in the covenant of the law.

But this first commandment is announced to people who must live their lives in a culture that worshiped many gods. Professor von Rad insists that this central fact is an important clue to an understanding of the first commandment. "The First Commandment takes for granted a polytheistic situation amongst those who are addressed" (von Rad, *Old Testament Theology*, p. 57). The polytheistic deification of the earth was a given expectation of the period 1290 B.C. Every culture with which the Jews were familiar was polytheistic in religious outlook. The matter was simply not up for discussion in the civilizations of Egypt, Babylon, or Canaan. Consequently, this commandment would be more culturally abrasive and startling in its own historical setting than in later historical periods of Western culture, which become more secular and less religious. But polytheism would last a long time. In fact, more than a thousand years after the law of Moses, the Roman historian Tacitus would criticize the strict monotheism of the Jews as "tasteless and mean" in contrast to the other religious movements of the first century. These were more lavish and lively with fascination concerning the pantheon of gods and divine forces they embraced. Tacitus would write:

The Egyptians worship many animals and images of monstrous form; the Jews have purely mental conceptions of Deity, as one in essence. They call those profane who make representations of God in human shape out of perishable materials. They believe that Being to be supreme and eternal, neither capable of representation, nor of decay. They therefore do not allow any images to stand in their cities, much less in their temples. This flattery is not paid to their kings, nor this honour to our Emperors. From the fact, however, that their priest used to chant to the music of flutes and cymbals, and to wear garlands of ivy, and that a golden vine was found in the temple, some have thought that they worshiped Father Liber, the conqueror of the East, though their institutions do not by any means harmonize with the theory; for Liber established a festive and cheerful worship, while the Jewish religion is tasteless and mean (*The Complete Works of Tacitus*, p. 660).

The first commandment therefore stands against the cultural expectations of 1290 B.C. This radical rejection of polytheism is drawn to its logical and most sweeping implications in the Shema of Deuteronomy 6: "Hear, O Israel: The Lord our God is one Lord, and you shall love the Lord your God with all your heart, and with all your soul, and with all your might." One God, not many! This is the teaching of the first commandment, according to the Shema.

Holy Intimacy

The oneness portrayed in the Shema is personal. Pierre Teilhard de Chardin describes this intense, uncompromising personhood of God as the "tenacious personalism" of holy intimacy. It is a direct personalism that challenges the impersonalness of our century as much as the polytheistic personalism of the century of Moses:

> To those who only know it outwardly, Christianity seems desperately intricate. In reality, taken in its main lines, it contains an extremely simple and astonishingly bold solution of the world.
>
> In the centre, so glaring as to be disconcerting, is the uncompromising affirmation of a personal God: God as providence, directing the universe with loving, watchful care; and God the revealer, communicating himself to man on the level of and through the ways of intelligence. It will be easy for me, after all I have said, to demonstrate the value and actuality of this tenacious personalism, not long since condemned as obsolete. The important thing to point out here is the way in which such an attitude in the hearts of the faithful leaves the door open to, and is easily allied to, everything that is great and healthy in the universal (Pierre Teilhard de Chardin, *The Phenomenon of Man*, pp. 292–93).

We have discovered first of all in the law that God is personal, and he is the one who can be known by human beings. Von Rad warns interpreters of the Law that it is impossible to understand the Ten Commandments if we neglect this intimate, personal relationship between Yahweh and Israel (von Rad, p. 56). The opening words of the Law establish this personal interpersonalness which becomes the living and integrating continuity throughout the Law.

The commandment announces our freedom from the false gods and the terrors connected to them because their "bluff has been called." There are not many gods, only one God. The air is cleared once and for all for those who trust the commandment. The commandment is therefore not only a warning; it is also the good news of liberation. When we trust the commandment, we are set free from the bad use of the religious instinct within each of us that searches for the lesser gods and godlike power formations to which we may give ourselves. We reach out toward different forms of ultimacy and seek to bring under our control that which we admire and fear most. But the tragedy of religion is that practices and rituals which we ourselves create, in order to establish contact with the ultimate, turn chaotic and destructively cruel.

Because we are all incurably religious, this religious instinct with all of its imaginative possibilities needs this healthy restraint of the first commandment. In the place of the gods and the "no gods" of human society, we are instead called to meet the God of character, "I am who I am," the God of event and word, the God of the covenant of the Law.

"You shall not make for yourself a graven image, or any likeness of anything that is in heaven above, or that is in the earth beneath, or that is in the water under the earth; you shall not bow down to them or serve them; for I the Lord your God am a jealous God, visiting the iniquity of the fathers upon the children to the third and fourth generation of those who hate me, but showing steadfast love to thousands of those who love me and keep my commandments" (Exodus 20:4–6).

The second commandment speaks directly to the problem of identity.

The word in the Old Testament Hebrew translated "graven image" becomes in the New Testament the Greek word translated "idol." In its literal sense the

Greek word means *shadow*. The word shadow captures the original Old Testament force in the word translated "graven image"—that creation of our religious impulse which is projected outward from ourselves and infused with special religious significance. An idol, therefore, is the attempt of a person or persons to find and project meanings that are inflated between their true size and significance. Our creativity as human beings is shown in the idols we have made; they show the imaginative possibilities of the human personality in that search for meaning. The Torah of God becomes as blunt and direct in the second commandment as in the first. We human beings find the meaning for our existence from our Creator Redeemer and nowhere else. In fact, when we reach out to something else and ask or insist that it grant this basic meaning to our lives, then we have created an idol. In that moment we have created our own signpost for the journey of our lives. We have assigned to that signpost a meaning that it does not intrinsically deserve.

God Speaks for Himself

First, let us understand the theological premise that undergirds this warning. The great presupposition of the Law is found in the Law's opening words. At the very center of all reality stands the God of character who speaks for himself, the God identified to us by the intense personal pronouns of the Law, and by the grand "I am who I am" disclosure to Moses at the burning bush. The same personal intensity that Abraham and Moses first experienced is now made known in the Law to the whole of Israel and through that ancient people to all people.

In the second commandment we hear a command that is focused more directly upon us and our journey experiences. It directly confronts the human need for a source from which to make sense of life. In this commandment we discover God's perspective on this human quest. We human beings have been made for relationship with God himself; therefore, to be fully human and to find out what it means to be a man or a woman, we need to be rightly related to our Creator.

Michelangelo portrayed this basic biblical principle in his theologically profound and artistically dramatic creation panel on the ceiling of the Sistine Chapel in Vatican City. The ceiling of this chapel, which contains one thousand square yards of frescos, depicts nine scenes from the Old Testament. Michelangelo began this great work in 1508 and completed his part of the panels in 1511. His portrayal of the creation of Adam is a masterpiece not only because of its artistic triumph, but because it also offers a theological statement about the meaning of the human creature.

Michelangelo's Adam is magnificent; he has a continuity with the earth and yet with all his powerful form and majesty, his hands are empty. With one hand he is searching and reaching out for more—he knows he is incomplete. This is the portrayal of a creature who is tempted to build idols in the quest for meaning because in the whole of creation it is man and woman who yearn for the answer to the question, "Who am I?"

Michelangelo's man is in the process of becoming human, and we are shown the intense and dramatic moment just before God touches his frame to make him man. The gap is insurmountable; only God is able to bridge the chasm between creation and Creator. The theological perspective of the artist is clear. Man does not become fully human apart from this relationship with the One who made him. What is also very clear is that when man, the human being, is touched by God, he does not become an angel or some hybrid form of super creature of the spiritual realm; he becomes mere man, mere woman, but man-woman made in the image of God.

There is no Gnosticism with its disdain for the body in Michelangelo's portrayal; he is not describing the creation of a spiritualized phantom-people. The artist has painted real persons who have a continuity with the earth. There is a mystery about this man in the central panel, both because of his obvious search for God and also because of God's love for him. The second commandment of the Law now grants the theological foundation to that search for meaning. Both the warnings and the promises of the second commandment show how volatile is the quest and how urgent it is that we in the human family find our meaning in the Lord of creation and nowhere else.

Questions We Must Confront

We must now ask several questions: How is it that a human being falls captive to graven images? How is it that persons and communities project onto particular objects or powers meanings that these objects and powers do not have? How is it that a fear arises toward these graven images with such total and devastating terror as we know is the case in the worship of idols?

These questions are both very old and very contemporary. They haunt Marlow in his journey to the jungle base of Kurtz in Joseph Conrad's *Heart of Darkness*. It is the question asked by the prophet Isaiah when he looks in distress at the confusion of people who have turned their lives over to that which is false and empty: "But when I look there is no one; among these there is no counselor who, when I ask, gives an answer. Behold, they are all a delusion; their works are nothing; their molten images are empty wind" (Isaiah 41:28–29).

What has happened in idolatry is that persons or communities reach out toward the created order itself and project their own strong expectations and fears upon parts or elements within that created existence. We create shadows and the shadow is thereby honored by misplaced worship; it is petitioned for benefits that it cannot fulfill. Finally, it is feared with the worst of all fear, the terror of emptiness—the yawning vacuum of shadows, the horror of sheer vacancy. It is this horror of emptiness that becomes the last words of Conrad's Kurtz: "O the horror, the horror!"

The second commandment uses the cosmology of the ancient world to make the command communicative: "Heaven, earth, water under the earth." These levels within the created order make the command clear that nothing in any part of the created order should receive human worship or become the basis for the projected images that attempt to resemble any part of that created existence. It means that the whole complex and diverse nature of the created order is included in this prohibition. There is nothing in heaven, that mysterious upward part of the created order (what Karl Barth calls "the creation inconceivable to us"), that deserves human worship. Thus to project a shadow in that direction is to seek the answer to the deepest questions from a source that is itself derivative and owes its own meanings to God.

The same warning applies to the search for meaning from the earth, the place of the contemporary (Karl Barth, "the creation conceivable to us"). There are no present tense political or religious leaders who deserve such recognition. When we assign to human leaders such great power we have succeeded only in fashioning an idol somewhat more contemporary and recognizable but nevertheless still not a worthy object for worship.

The warning also applies to the downward side of the cosmological mystery of creation. There are no powers in the realms of death that should hold sway over human life or conscience. This realm, frightful as it is, is still a part of the larger whole of the created order, and therefore it in no sense deserves our fears and certainly not our worship.

Idol-making can become a very intricate process in which a positive value like the love of the family or nation is twisted into an ideal that often will justify acts of injustice toward the neighbor who is of another national or family group. This distortion of values has resulted in the most terrifying forms of evil in our twentieth century. Socio-religious-political idolatry has been the graven image of the earth for each generation of human beings and the results have always been corrosive. "The Great Masquerade of evil has played havoc with all of our ethical concepts" (Dietrich Bonhoeffer, *Letters and Papers from Prison*, p. 94).

The Jealous God?

The commandment identifies God as the jealous God. This word is powerfully humanlike in its connotation. We

47

should not be surprised at this humanness, because the personalness of the Torah has already been established in the first commandment and in the preface to the Law. The word "jealous" means to care intimately about the event taking place so that a strong reaction is promised. In this context the word jealous means that God is the One who cares deeply about the events that take place, and he promises a response—either judgment or blessing. The blessing is stronger and more far-reaching—"thousands" of generations—whereas the judgment is assigned to the third and fourth generations. Even in the warning grace is stronger than judgment!

What we have are two commandments and two great presuppositions of biblical faith and life. These have been affirmed in the Law. First we have found the great Abrahamic and Mosaic discovery—God is personal. The second is related to the first. We who are persons find the meaning of our existence in God and nowhere else. The commands are stern, but they are both good news.

"You shall not take the name of the Lord your God in vain" (Deuteronomy 5:11). This third commandment alerts us to the importance of the holy name of God. Great attention is given to names in the life of Israel and in the New Testament church as well. The name of a person was understood as an expression of the person's unique character. (See the discussion of names and naming in Old Testament tradition in Bernhard W. Anderson's *Understanding the Old Testament*, p. 52. "In the thought of ancient Israel . . . it was believed that the name was filled with power and vitality." This helps us understand why powerful life experiences would result in the renaming of a person (i.e., Genesis 32:27–28).) Because of this cultural

attention to names the term *name* in the third commandment is used in this precise and highly significant sense. It
is the very character and self-disclosure of God's character as he has made himself known to us that is carried in
the Name of the Holy One.

The verb translated, "take in vain," is the crucial
term that we must understand in order to really make
sense of this commandment. The most obvious meaning of
this term in the Hebrew language is "to empty," or "to
make empty." Professor von Rad explains, however, that
another meaning lies just beneath the surface of this interesting word: "It is probably that the word which we translate as 'in vain' might at a very early period have meant
'magic'" (von Rad, p. 57).

At this point we must make a few technical observa-
tions about the study of the Ten Commandments in terms
of their place in the Old Testament text. If the interpreter
of the Ten Commandments agrees with the consensus of
nineteenth-century Old Testament criticism and places
the time of writing of these words at a late date, as, for
example, the time of the Prophets, then our linguistic
interest from a technical standpoint is focused upon the
literature and writing methods of the late or early
prophetic period—from about 750 B.C. to about 400 B.C.
But we now know that the Jewish language was formed
and active much earlier than the form-critical scholars of
the nineteenth century had imagined. Therefore we are
confronted with a whole new task and exciting possibility
for the understanding of documents such as the Exodus,
Deuteronomy presentations of the Ten Commandments
which, by their position in the Old Testament, claim early
authorship. If in fact this document was written by Moses

at or near the date 1290–1250 B.C., the word in the commandment, *YHWH* (Yahweh), is understood as an old word, not as the linguistic invention of prophetic writers some 600 years later.

History Speaks

This shift in balance in Old Testament linguistic study has produced a whole new interest in the formation and development of the Hebrew language. The recent archaeological discoveries at Ebla, at Tell Mardikh in Syria, are of tremendous importance in this inquiry. They have given to modern scholars the opportunity to search out some examples of early, concrete, daily-use meanings of Hebrew words. These, in addition to other archaeological evidences of early Semitic literacy, such as the Sumerian prism and the Code of Hammurabi, have moved all dates for the actual authorship of books in the Old Testament to earlier periods. The traditional Jewish understanding of the authorship of Old Testament books is now more reasonable and faithful to the evidence than most of the elaborate theories that were dogmatically asserted by the form-critical scholars of the nineteenth and early twentieth centuries. Those critics, who dominated Old Testament studies with their dismissal of the possibility of Mosaic authorship of the books of the law, have now been strongly challenged by the evidence of language itself.

What does all this mean for our study of the word choice "in vain" in the third commandment? It means that this word is old, and we therefore want to face its old meanings as well as its later meanings. In its later development the word carries the sense of "empty." We are commanded against any carelessness on our part toward the holy meaning of the one who God is in his person-hood; such carelessness might lead us into emptying the holy name of God of its content. We now know from von Rad's research into the older period of the Hebrew word that it also carries within it the sense of "magic." This means that the third commandment warns against the vanity not only of emptiness but also of sorcery and magic. Both kinds of vanity are destructive because both diminish the name of the Lord.

Now let us look more closely at the word. *Shw* is the Hebrew word, and its concrete root meaning is "empty pit." This word is also the word for "ruin," "devastation." One of the verb forms of this word means to pervert, to ruin, to make something empty. An interesting use of this word is found in 1 Samuel 28:3–9, where the witch of Endor is described as having the spirit of the "hollow sound." This same word, *shw*, is the word that now appears in the third commandment.

How are we to understand the commandment? First, we are commanded not to pervert or profane the name of the Lord. This is what happens when the good name of God is reversed so that the name of love becomes the means of curse. What happens in profanity is that the name of the holy and righteous God is used as a term of ruin and devastation. Someone or something is damned by the name of the holy One who was first identified to us as the Redeemer! What an ironic twist and perversion!

We are also commanded not to empty the name of God with the hollow flattery of adoration which is not matched by the reality of discipleship. In this case the name of God is used and even honored—at least apparently—but the praise is actually emptied by the unwillingness to act out the words we speak. This emptying is the milder form of the word *shw*, but it can be equally destructive because of its built-in self-deception. We are tempted to think that because we have *spoken* the words we have therefore *done* what we have spoken. Jesus put it this way in his own commentary on the Law: "Not every one who says to me Lord, Lord, shall enter the kingdom of heaven, but he who does the will of my Father" (Matthew 7:21).

We are also commanded not to practice sorcery or any form of magic arts, though they may be designed to enable us to make contact with God or with some other spiritual reality. Like the advice of the witch of Endor, they are the counsel of the "hollow sound." We have no need of the magician or religious guru because God is able to speak for himself. The signposts along the pathway of our life do not require the decoding skill of witchcraft. They are clear and plain in themselves.

Now the question we must ask is this. If we are not to empty the name of the Lord in any of these three ways, then what are we to do? What is the opposite of "to empty"? Psalm 119, the psalm of the law, faces this very question by its practical affirmations:

> Teach me, O Lord, the way of thy statutes;
>   and I will keep it to the end.
> Give me understanding, that I may keep thy law
>   and observe it with my whole heart.
> Lead me in the path of thy commandment,
>   for I delight in it.
> Incline my heart to thy testimonies,
>   and not to gain!

Turn my eyes from looking at vanities;
and give me life in thy ways (119:33–37).

Joy Davidman has caught the essence of this psalm and the positive intention of the third commandment in her comments on this commandment. She states it in positive terms: "Thou shalt take the Name of the Lord thy God in earnest! . . . It is high time" (*Smoke on the Mountain,* p. 47).

What does it mean to trust God? What does it mean in the century in which I now live?

First, we meet the God of character who can be trusted, known, and loved. He is the one personal God.

Second, we are confronted with the fact that the meaning of existence is to be found in God himself and nowhere else.

Third, God is the One who discloses his own character and makes himself known. He speaks for himself and therefore we have no need for magicians or our own empty phrases. We have only to listen earnestly.

-4-

Love

During the summer of 1985 my family and I fulfilled a life-long dream and took the Trans-Siberian train across the Soviet Union. Our train trip began in Beijing, China, and ended in Helsinki, Finland. One of the highlights of that journey was the city of Leningrad in the USSR, and three places in that city meant the most to us. First, we saw the Dostoevsky house, the flat where Fyodor Dostoevsky wrote the book *Brothers Karamazov* and where he died. We also saw St. Isaac's Cathedral and its marvelous wall murals of biblical scenes.

The third place impressed us the most. We spent one day in the vast palace of Catherine the Great, *The Hermitage*, which is now the home for one of the world's greatest art collections. This collection is so extensive that there are in that one museum more Rembrandt paintings than in any other museum in the world (even in Holland). We were escorted through this 1,000-room museum by a very knowledgeable Intourist guide who explained to us in detail the history and significance of the paintings.

I did not feel we needed her descriptions as much when we came to the Rembrandt collection, because Rembrandt has been a hero of mine for quite a long time. Nevertheless I listened closely to each explanation she made of the paintings.

The greatest painting in the Rembrandt rooms is his

final unfinished painting, "Return of the Prodigal." In this painting the Prodigal Son is kneeling before his father and the great kindly hands of the father are resting gently upon the shoulders of his runaway son, now home. There is in all of art no portrayal of hands as emotionally and intellectually compelling as those great liberating hands of the father in this painting.

Our guide told us of the hands and of the history of this final painting by the great painter and then she said, "Notice how the blind father is blessing his son." I was startled and thought I had misunderstood her words, so I asked her to repeat what she had said. "Notice how the blind father is blessing his son." I was totally shocked, so I dared to challenge our very self-confident guide and reminded her of the key elements of the parable of Jesus which is the basis for Rembrandt's painting—precisely the whole point of this parable turns upon how excellent the father's eyesight really is, "While the boy was a long way off the father saw him and had compassion and ran to him. . . ."

The very drama of this parable rests upon the discovery of the son by the father and the merciful act of the father which catches everyone by surprise. From the perspective of the story of Jesus the turning point of the parable is that the father *saw* his lost son. Fortunately for the Prodigal, it is the father who saw him before the elder brother, because we know from the final lines of the story that had his older brother discovered him first, he might not have made it home at all.

Our guide did not insist upon her earlier explanation after I quoted these few lines from the parable by Jesus. Later when we were alone together as a family, we began to talk about the incredible experience we had had in front of the Rembrandt painting.

During our trek in The Hermitage our guide had told us that her specialty as an Intourist guide had been to escort American student groups. I do not know how many years she had been with Intourist carrying out this assignment, but what astounded me was that she had probably described this painting to Intourist groups on numerous tours through The Hermitage with the same interpretive sentence which she had told us: "Notice the blind father as he blesses his son." Evidently until she had met up with our group no one had previously challenged that interpretation of the painting!

The Absence of Knowledge

Allan Bloom's *The Closing of the American Mind* helped me to understand how such a thing could be possible. He has one line in this book in which he observes that American students do not enjoy the art museums of Europe as much as they should because they don't know the Bible and most of the masterworks in the galleries of Europe require such a knowledge. But something more significant for ourselves and for our culture is involved in this absence of knowledge than the ability to make sense of art exhibits.

I realized that our generation cannot assume that because we live in this time and place where Bibles are openly available that we know and understand the great themes of the Bible—not even this greatest of themes as found in the Parable of the Prodigal Son of Luke 15. Our generation—students included—needs to know and experience the vast love that Rembrandt's painting portrays in the hands and face of the father toward the exhausted figure of this prodigal son now come home. We need to know St. Luke's account of the words of Jesus. It is very important to us in our pilgrimage experience that we know the true source and the quality of this love as it comes from the great Storyteller himself, Jesus Christ.

The blessing in Rembrandt's painting is not a generalized kindness nor is it a blessing received by the deception of a crafty prodigal, as was the case of the shrewd Jacob and his elderly father, Isaac. This is quite a different story that Jesus has told in his greatest parable. The father in Christ's parable sees very well and knows how to find both of his sons. He sees the younger son while he is a great distance away and finds this son broken and humiliated. But later in that story while a celebration is underway this same father walks out into the night to find his other lost and angry son, the elder brother. We need to know about this love that Jesus has portrayed for us in his parable because it is the very love that Jesus Christ has granted to us in his life, death, and resurrection. He, the storyteller, is the father who finds us when we are lost, either through defeat or through self-righteous anger. He is the one who sets us free and who pays the price for our freedom. This love is the value better than any other value—and the one upon which all other values depend.

A Mist of Misinterpretation

The art gallery incident is itself something like a parable within a parable. It tells the story of many people who do not experience the love of God because somehow they do not see it in front of their eyes. Or what they see, *and* how they interpret what they see, is a picture that almost tells the true story but not really.

There is a mist of misinterpretation that creates a disastrous blur of fundamental colors and shades. When this happens we become a people who do not know the life and ministry of Jesus of Nazareth well enough to understand his grace. The result is that we may think of God's love in the terms of the guide's interpretation as the reward for our skillful deception; we feel this way because we cannot imagine any love that would be granted to the real person that I am. "If the Father could really see who I am and what I am really like, how could he love me?" When such a foglike confusion happens, the result is that we become disoriented from every other subject too. Surely, we need to read this signpost clearly or we will miss every other signpost because this one lies at the beginning of the whole journey.

If I know about the love of God as Jesus Christ has revealed that love, both in the parable and most of all in his ministry, in his sacrifice, and in his victory, then I will be on the right pathway. If I do not know of this grace or if I have a confused understanding of it, then I am lost at the beginning. I become like the tour guide with only half the story in my mind and life.

The discovery of God's grace is the most fundamental of all human discoveries—and the most important basis for the wisdom skills that enable a man or woman to find the way in the journey. This discovery of the love of Jesus Christ is itself a growing experience that takes a lifetime of discipleship to fully comprehend. From the very earliest moments in which the truth of Christ's grace dawns upon our lives, however, we are on the right pathway. The discovery has everything to do with our brains as we need to learn who Jesus really is. And it has everything to do with our hearts as we need to respond to his love and really believe that it is intended for us.

Once the love of God is in my life, it has become a value to live for and to live from. It becomes in my life the greatest source of motivation. Because Jesus Christ is not a theoretical principle but the living Lord, his love is a daily companionship as well in the streets where I live, and the art galleries too.

-5-

The Balanced Life

Here is another marker that everyone endorses and very few follow: *Keep your balance*. Balance is fundamental in every athletic event, and it is just as fundamental for every ordinary life event. The problem of imbalance is always on our minds when we hear stories about other people's burnout or stress-related illness. The difficulty is our problem when we find our own stomach burning not because of bad food but because of imbalanced lifestyle. This marker along the roadway is just the value signpost that we need. Most people, however, are quite surprised when they discover that very early in the Bible the question of balance was thought of at a very deep level and with considerable wisdom. The fourth commandment is a good place to begin building an understanding of the biblical portrayal of balance:

> Observe the sabbath day to keep it holy as the Lord your God commanded you. Six days you shall labor, and do all your work; but the seventh day is a sabbath to the Lord your God; in it you shall not do any work, you, or your son, or your daughter, or your manservant, or your maidservant, or your ox, or your ass, or any of your cattle, or the sojourner who is within your gates, that your manservant and your maidservant may rest as well as you. You shall remember that you were a servant in the land of Egypt, and the Lord your God brought you out thence with a mighty hand and an outstretched arm; therefore

the Lord your God commanded you to keep the sabbath day (Deuteronomy 5:12–15).

The word *sabbath* in this text is one of the few Hebrew words that have been transliterated directly into English usage without translation. The three other best-known words are hallelujah, which translates as "praise the Lord"; hosanna, which translates as "please help"; and amen, which means "faithful." Sabbath is the Hebrew root for several Old Testament words. Its literal meaning is "cease," but it is also a root word for words translated "seven" and "rest."

The presentation of this commandment in Deuteronomy contains several sentences not found in the Exodus 20 text where the Ten Commandments are also stated. "You shall remember . . . ." This added sentence more concretely unites the fourth commandment to the first commandment and to the preface of the Ten Commandments. The Exodus text of the fourth commandment relates the sabbath commandment to creation; the Deuteronomy text relates the Sabbath to redemption.

What Does It Mean?

We must ask the question, What is the meaning of this commandment? What does it teach us about life in addition to what it commands? It is important to notice that the fourth commandment offers an interpretation of the ordinary day-to-day living of human beings and the world they occupy. A unit of time, namely seven days, is used as a framework within which we are able to think about ourselves and our work, our relationships, our worship, our rest. Man and woman are not assessed in terms of their relationship to a year or a month or a day but to a week. Not only that, but the week is understood in terms of an intrinsic and dynamic rhythm of work and rest.

What does this description of the human being and his or her world teach? From it we learn that we are so designed that we need to work and to rest, to act and to be, to run and to walk. The portrayal is rhythmic, and human life is pictured within the context of an essential balance.

We are creatures who need to stop and think, to worship and rest, to work hard when we work, to play when we play, and pause when we pause. We need unhurried time within the balance of the seven ordinary days to collect our thoughts and to remember who we are. We need to remember the fact of the goodness of creation and the redemptive love of God that found us when we were in bondage. The interpretation of personhood that emerges in the Torah includes this rhythmic week as an essential ingredient of humanness. It is presented not as a desirable possibility for the affluent but as the essential mark for all humankind, and thus it is mandated.

In other words, from the perspective of the Torah we human beings are designed to live a rhythmic week; we function best in the wise and good rhythm of work and rest, time alone and time in community, *in*tensive and *ex*tensive experiences, physical exercise and mental reflection. This is the view of life that is being taught in the commandment.

In the context of this seven-day framework, it becomes the role of the fourth commandment to affirm the universal relevance of this "law of balance." The essential balance of the rhythmic week is God's gift not only for men but also for women, not only for Jewish citizens but also for sojourners (foreign travelers and visitors), not only for the human family in creation, but also for animals.

In the later extension of the law, this rhythmic principle will be applied in many other directions. For example, the land itself will benefit from this commandment: "For six years you shall sow your land and gather in its yield; but the seventh year you shall let it rest and lie fallow, that the poor of your people may eat; and what they leave the wild beasts may eat" (Exodus 23:10–11). Institutions are to be rhythmic as well—for example, the concept of the jubilee year of social redistribution of wealth after seven times seven years (Leviticus 25).

The law has in its way paid to man and woman (and the created order they occupy) a rich compliment. Human beings are not mechanical, timeless creatures who can grind on endlessly at work. We need quality time to collect our thoughts and our dreams. We also need time to "cease" and to wonder about the deep meanings of life. And we need to remember our history and to worship the Lord of life. We need work, too, with its creative productivity and energy. Though the fourth commandment is an imperative, it is an imperative that leads me toward true freedom of balance.

It also leads to dominion. In the first chapter of the Bible (Genesis 1:26), man and woman are granted dominion over the earth. This dominion text becomes the beginning of the freedom theology of the Bible. Now, in the fourth commandment of the Law, that dominion thread is once again affirmed. The fourth commandment tells us to choose the good way within the seven-day cycle that describes our lives. We are the ones who choose the work and we choose the rest—and we are given that dominion by this mandate. We are to find our work and our rest; that is to say, we are given the responsibility to think through the meaning of our life within the seven days each of us has to live in a particular week. The commandment is therefore concerned with the positive framework of work and rest given by God through men and women as a gift to the created order for our good, and the good of the whole of creation.

What Does Jesus Say?

During his ministry Jesus confronted more confusion and antagonisms concerning the fourth commandment than all the rest of the Law. Most of that confusion and opposition centered on the meaning of the gift of the "cease" day, the day of rest. Ironically, this gift had become a misunderstood and totally legalized battlefield of argument and stress by the time of the first century. The Essenes would prove their own ascetic superiority over the Pharisees by insisting upon more stringent "cease" regulations than the Pharisee lawyers could justify. An example of this is found in Jesus' challenge to the Pharisees in Matthew 12:11 concerning the man who helped a lamb out of a pit on the sabbath. This question points up a difference of extremity between Pharisee interpreters and the hard-line sabbatarianism of the Qumran sect. The Qumran sect held, "No one should help an animal to foal on the sabbath day. And if it should drop [its foal] into a pit or well, let no one raise it on the sabbath day" (H. H. Rowley, "Zadokitework" in *From Moses to Qumran*, p. 251). In this Sabbatarianism we see the evidence of harsh technical interpretation that is totally devoid of either compassion or common sense. This law of the good balance had become so much the technical specialty of the religious lawyers that most of its ethical richness and human atmosphere had been contaminated by the severity of self-righteous one-upmanship. Jesus does not hesitate to challenge this serious distortion of the original gospel intention of the Torah. One of the most dramatic confrontations concerning the fourth commandment is recorded for us by Mark:

> Again he entered the synagogue, and a man was there who had a withered hand. And they watched him, to see whether he would heal him on the sabbath, so that they might accuse him. And he said to the man who had the withered hand, "Come here." And he said to them, "Is it lawful on the sabbath to do good or to do harm, to save life or to kill?" But they were silent. And he looked around at them with anger, grieved at their hardness of heart and said to the man, "Stretch out your hand." He stretched it out, and his hand was restored. The Pharisees went out, and immediately held counsel with the Herodians against him, how to destroy him (Mark 3:1–6).

Notice how Jesus in this very important confrontation focuses attention upon the goodness of the fourth commandment and its healthy purpose. The tragedy of this narrative is that his listeners are firmly entrenched in their own legalism and fear. The result for them of this anxious technical fascination with the correct definition of work and rest is a hardness and joylessness that is totally foreign to the generous design of the commandment.

They missed the obvious truth that both in our work and in our rest we are to do good, not harm.

The other half of the rhythm is work; six days we are to work. The logic of the commandment is clear; rest without work is nonrhythmic just as work without rest is nonrhythmic. Each needs its companion gift to be truly humanizing. When work and rest are united, we have a stewardship view of life. The fourth commandment looks at our individual lives, and the lives of the created order that surround us, in terms of health and balance. This commandment grants to us the dominion, which means the responsibility, for care of ourselves and the earth. We are not to exploit ourselves on the earth or those who work for us, but we are to do good by the tasks of our work and by the reflective pauses of our rest. The doctrine of work brings us into a dynamic and creative relationship with the earth as we make use of the unique giftedness in our stewardship responsibility. The six days of labor earn the money to support the family and to provide resources for good works, and make it possible for the family to rest. There is therefore in the Sabbath commandment an economic equanimity as well as a psychological and sociological balance.

Work Is Good . . . and Hard

But work is work and there is no easy way to do it, whether it is feeding livestock, learning complicated mathematical equations, doing serious Bible study, or typing manuscripts. For some people there is no easy way to rest either—but work is still harder because it lasts longer (at least during our lifetime). There are six days of work to the one day of rest in the balanced week of our earthly existence. Work is good and it has many spiritual and physical benefits, but work, by definition, is hard.

Recently I had a conversation with three wranglers who were in charge of the horses at one of the InterVarsity Ranch camps in Alberta, Canada. We were talking about the horses and the very cold weather of Alberta during the winter. I made the ignorant observation, "You keep the horses in barns during the winter months, don't you?"

The wranglers enjoyed the next few minutes telling me that, quite to the contrary, the horses stayed outside during the winter. "We have trees on the range where they keep out of the worst wind."

I was amazed and followed up my first question with what I thought was a reasonable second question: "But you don't ride them in the winter, do you?"

They were also cheered by this question as they assured me that the horses loved to be ridden in the winter at below-zero temperatures. One final sentence really struck me. "Of course, after every ride it is very important to walk them around and completely wipe them down so their sweat doesn't chill them."

It was then I realized that wrangling horses at thirty degrees below zero was hard work, and not everyone was up to it. Perhaps it has been the western films that have made a cowboy's life seem so carefree and almost casual. The fact is that all work is very hard some of the time. Nevertheless, if it is honest work it should be good. "Sweat is one thing that money can't buy."

A good criterion pervades the fourth commandment. The good result of work, in addition to the task completed, is that through hard work we are enabled to develop our full stride as human beings. It is through work that a young man or woman develops the skills and talents of his or her particular uniqueness. Both rest and work help us to feel good about ourselves, not only about our hearts but also about our hands, not only about what we think and feel but also about what we do and what we can make.

A rhythmic stride emerges from work and rest that confirms our humanity, and that stride should continue throughout our lives until the day we die. The Bible does not have a doctrine of retirement; rather, what the Bible advocates is a doctrine of discipleship with generational and time-adjusted variations in the kinds of work and rest we are to choose and do. It is harmful to superimpose upon people an artificial expectation that at a certain arbitrary age they should "retire" and from that point on live nonrhythmically. Such an expectation is dangerous to mental and spiritual—and even physical—health. We are to work and to rest in rhythmic balance, if possible, right up to the end of our lives. The work may evolve through several fascinating careers and opportunities of stewardship and service, but work and rest must accompany each other throughout the journey.

The commandment lays the responsibility upon each one of us, directly and personally. We must find both our work and our rest. Some of the time we may develop the expectation that others must force us to rest, and in some cases that other people must find work for us to do. The commandment does not encourage such an expectation. As a pastor, I often meet parishioners who will say to me, "I am willing to be of service, but no one in the church has asked me to help out." To these people the text says,

"You must find your work; it is there to do. Be creative and research the needs; if you do not find it, that is your problem."

The point of the commandment is that a stewardship obligation is being affirmed. Other people I meet are, by choice, workaholics. Sometimes they are secretly proud of the fact that they have mercilessly burned the candles of their lives at every place a wick was visible. But the commandment lays upon them the obligation to balance their lives for the good of the earth and for their own good. They must find their rest because a burned out and burned up hard working man or woman is not in God's intention for human life.

Though this fact of inescapable personal obligation is true in the commandment, it is also true that one of the finest gifts we can share with other people is to help them find their work and their balance between rest and work. When young people are enabled to get started in the working world, a substantial contribution has been made toward their sense of well-being. Self-confidence is greatly influenced by how a person succeeds in the working half of the rhythm. The fourth commandment does not attach an inordinate importance to work as the indicator of worth or personal significance; rather, it places weight upon the principle of balanced wholeness. We have here the beginnings of a *shalom* theology, the theology of health and integration.

Two More Themes

We must now develop two more theological themes that are important ingredients of the fourth commandment. First, this commandment shows us that nothing goes on and on without interruption. There are limits built into God's design concerning our life, our authority, and our responsibility. This commandment treats life in terms of a concrete boundary; the segment of seven days has a beginning and an ending because of God's good decision. The boundary which limits our work is not a punishment but has the same kind of theological significance as the Genesis portrayal of the six days of creation. Each day is drawn to a close and is weighed and measured and valued by the stated opinion of God—"he saw that it was good." It is good that history has boundaries; it is good that our work fits within a context of meaning. It is good that God's decision stands at the beginning and at the end of everything, including our own seven-day cycles.

But the most profound truth hidden within this commandment has to do with the meaning of the seventh day as a sign of the movement of the human tide toward the messianic fulfillment of history. The seventh day concludes the week in the same way as in the grand account of creation—the seventh day is the day without an ending, the day that belongs to God, on which he rested. From a theological viewpoint this may explain why our Lord consciously and deliberately asserted his own authority over the day of rest in his controversial encounters with religious opinion-makers of the first century concerning the proper observation of the sabbath. Jesus announces his messiahship in the context of the Sabbath with the bold sentence, "I tell you, something greater than the temple is here. . . . For the Son of man is Lord of the sabbath" (Matthew 12:1–8).

St. Augustine was convinced that the real significance of the sabbath is this very fact: the seventh day provides a concrete sign of fulfillment toward which history yearns; because of the grace and decision of God, human history moves toward that fulfillment symbolized by the seventh day. He opened and concluded his *Confessions* with variations on this thought: "Thou madest us for thyself, and our heart is restless until it repose in thee" (p. 3). "O Lord God, give peace unto us . . . the peace of rest, the peace of the Sabbath, which hath no evening . . . thou, Lord, ever workest, and art ever at rest" (p. 337).

This is the rhythm—"ever at work, ever at rest." God's meaning in Jesus Christ has permanently changed everything for the better: "Do little things as though they were great, because of the majesty of Jesus Christ who does them in us, and who lives our life, and do the greatest things as though they were little and easy, because of His omnipotence" (Pascal, *Pensées*, #552).

-6-

Family

Let me show you what a family is. It happens something like this: Without our prior consent, each of us is entrusted—physically, spiritually, and emotionally—to an interpersonal, amateur institution. Those in charge are usually young and have little or no experience. They are called parents. By our birth or by adoption, we enter and are so completely immersed within its support and discipline for the first years of our lives that our very physical survival depends upon this ancient though inexperienced institution, the family.

Later on, in our adolescence, we are gradually loosened from the family's discipline with some or all forms of its support so that in young adulthood the human being who once was the baby in everyone's arms now stands separately. This goes on just long enough for most humans to make the choice that voluntarily joins them up again with this very ancient interpersonal fellowship called marriage and the family. When this decision is agreed to by another whom we love, then the incredible cycle of human birth and becoming starts over again.

Why the Family?

The question I want to ask is this: Why does this institution called the family exist in God's creation and redemption design? The inescapable conclusion that makes the most sense to me is this: "God decided that what a man or a woman must have to become truly human develops best of all in a family. This means that the family takes its part as a critical link in the order of creation—and it also takes its part as an important link in the order of redemption. Jesus himself taught about families and he especially told parables about the family; his stories fit together with other biblical teaching to become for us a portrait of his high view of the family's significance for people-building.

The parables are always realistic, and they are always encouraging too. One of the most fascinating of these parables is the brief story Jesus tells in the Sermon on the Mount: "If a son ask for bread will his father give him a rock, if a fish will his father give him a serpent . . . ?" (Matthew 7). In this parable, Jesus creates for us a model in which we learn about the purpose of parenting. We exist as parents to give good gifts to our children; and even though we may have our own problems, we still try to fulfill that purpose: "Even though sinful you know how to give good gifts to your children" (Matthew 7:11). The parable is not only intended by Jesus as an illustration of the goodness of the Father who is the greatest father, but it also reveals to us an expectation from Jesus about the mission of ordinary human parents. We now know that it is Christ's will that we give bread and fish, not a stone or serpent, to our own children. We also know that this gift-giving happens in ordinary families and less than perfect families since even sinful fathers and mothers give good gifts. The question I want to ask is this: What is the "bread" and "fish" that human beings need to receive from mothers and fathers? What nourishment is the family best of all equipped to offer to the emerging young men and women in its midst?

There are at least five essential marks of humanness that are best communicated to us in families. Each of these is a food needed as nourishment in the early stages of growing just as each is mysteriously involved as the raw material building blocks of the experience of redemption in the middle stages of our growing up as human beings.

1) The first is *language* that bears a unique identity imprint and accent. Language is best learned in a family, and not only is this a linguistic event but it is much more. It is language with the special accent and hidden family cues and sayings that converge to form me into a unique person. The proof from the order of creation that God wanted his human creatures to be special and individually fascinating is found in his decision to entrust our language formation primarily to parents and grandparents, brothers and sisters. Thus, we need the family to help us know how to speak and to hear.

2) *Culture* is best taught in families, and this is a second need that brings us to our parents and grandparents, relatives near and far, to ask for bread and fish. Culture is the mixture of shared memory that we sometimes call tradition, together with the reasons we have that explain to us the past and present. The family, with its photo albums and acted-out ceremonies of belonging, takes on this tremendously important role in our lives. It is the family's task to try to explain our existence so that as persons we feel worthwhile and necessary in a long continuum of significance. We are looking for a bread

that says we not only have histories but a history as well. We have a name that describes both our belonging and our uniqueness.

3) *Meaning* is the dynamic coming together of the values of daily habits and future goals. Meaning is the substantial bread shared in the family when we learn together how to make practical decisions on the basis of long-term purposes and agreed-upon convictions. This happens or "half happens" first of all in a family.

4) *Faith* is also first learned when we are very young. We trust our parents, and we believe what they tell us especially in the earliest years of our lives when we believe mothers and fathers without any questions. We discover that faith is a journey experience that must find its sources and faithful testing ground through the traveling together in which we meet up with assurance as well as disappointment, with doubt as well as realistic confidence. The family takes this journey with us.

5) Finally, it is in the family that we first meet up with *love*. Just moments after our birth, we find love in the embrace of our mother and then our father, brothers and sisters, grandparents. From the beginning love in a family is the celebration of who I am right now as a person, so that there is nothing I can do to earn or achieve it. Just being who I am is enough! It is love that nourishes the person that I am so that I feel good about being alive.

Essential Food

Each of these five ingredients is essential food for every human being. In a thousand ways before we ask anyone else we ask our parents for these five foods as the bread and fish for our lives. It is all part of the grand design of God. Because of the vital significance of these five markers of humanness it is clear that each of us has a profound stake in all families; the health of every family, in one way or another, has an impact upon our lives. Healthy families that learn to speak and listen, to celebrate history and make righteous decisions, to trust and to love, are a benefit to all other families. It is also true that every one of us is affected when any daughter or son receives a rock instead of bread, or a snake instead of a fish, from the very ones who were mandated by God's purpose in creation to give good gifts to their children.

Our task as human beings ourselves is clear; each one of us must help every family to give good gifts to the next generation of human beings. We must be at work at all times with the nourishment of good gift-giving in families and with the redeeming good news of help for the family that has become entangled in rocks and snakes. When we follow and trust Jesus Christ we discover the richness of the bread of the gospel and that deepens even more our stake. Youth ministry, in the Christian church, is therefore at its heart, a ministry to families as much as it is a ministry to youth themselves. Those who minister in Christ's church can never forget that commitment to the whole person who is young and vulnerable.

What about each of us and our own ancient institution? How do I as the member of a family give the good gifts I want to give? There is one ingredient that is necessary for each of these fine foods of the soul to happen: language, culture, meaning, faith, and love. That one ingredient is *presence*. If you are a father or mother, you first of all must be at the place where your son or daughter can find you in order for them to ask about the bread and fish. Personal presence takes time, and there is no nourishment of the soul without it. Some families spend hours in proximity to each other and, yet, have very little real presence to go with the proximity. When I use the word "presence," I mean time together in which real language and real listening takes place so that memories are created out of the ordinary and decisions are made, faith is begun, and love is happening through us. Time/presence is the focused gift we give to each other. In a family, it means that there is *time* for you—time for you to ask for help, time to be yourself, to relax, to cry, to laugh, to argue about ideas, to tell stories that other people outside of our family might not be interested in. Here is your safe place where you are important so that even when time is short and when people are very busy, the principle still holds true that there are times you do have together than can be *presence* time. This presence cannot happen *all* the time, but it needs to happen *some* of the time, enough of the time so that we are able to grow our character. Theologically, there is a larger reality behind this too. What God has given to each of us that is more important than any other gift is his own presence alongside and within our lives. "If you then know how to give good gifts to your children . . . how much more your heavenly father."

In the divine master plan the family is that kingdom within all other kingdoms where these roadway signs of life meanings (that every human being must have) are taught and discovered: culture, purpose, faith, and love. This presence of real people brought together to create a family is the mystery of the ancient institution that had its start in a man and woman who were strongly attracted to each other, fell in love, and, because of promises they each made to one another decided to live together. Marriage creates family, and children enlarge the family. But two make a family, and if through divorce or death the original marriage partnership is changed nevertheless the family as a reality remains.

The Newest Ones Alive

The family exists chronologically as, first of all, the communion of a man and a woman. The family is God's intention as the source of new life so that to these two adults may be granted in God's wisdom the stewardship of the newest ones alive.

The newest ones alive are called children; because they are born so small they need the special protection of parental adults when they are very young, and every year on their birthday they need adults to celebrate who they are. As children grow up through the tender years of childhood, they continue to need from adults total care, education, encouragement, and physical and emotional protection. Adolescence is the most dynamic part of the journey with its own growing momentum for the young person who is now emerging into adulthood. Nevertheless, it also produces its own kind of vulnerability and therefore youth still need the discipline, understanding, education, protection, and respect of the adults who share with them their teen years. This is how human beings are made, and this caring journey is God's design for the pilgrimage from birth to the full stride of young adulthood. At each turn of the road and change of grade on that pilgrimage route, there are different kinds of vulnerabilities and hazards that a growing child encounters. There are thus different kinds of opportunities and positive moments for the encouragement and blessing of the boy or girl we call the newest one alive.

When we read the Bible, we know that children are so highly valued by God that there are songs to celebrate their birth, such as Hannah's song (1 Samuel 2:1–10); there are also ceremonies, (such as circumcision in the Old Testament and infant baptism in the New) in which families claim the covenant promises of God for their children. Added to these positive signs of God's will for our children are the grave warnings of Jesus Christ the Lord against any men or women who would cause one of his littlest ones to stumble. The warning is as clear as it is stern: "It would be better for him to have a great millstone fastened round his neck and to be drowned in the depth of the sea" (Matthew 18:6).

The protection of children begins in the Old Testament as the people of Israel were commanded by God not to harm their children in religious rites as was the custom in the religious practices of Baal and Asherah. Israel was commanded especially to provide for children who are without parents (the orphans and the widows always receive special protective provision in the Law and the Prophets of the Old Testament). The ancient cultures that surrounded Israel practiced child sacrifice to fertility gods, but in the Old Testament the horrible practice of Molech (child sacrifice as a religious act) was called an abomination by God. King Ahab and King

Zedekiah, for example, were condemned by the God of Israel for practicing that act (1 Kings 16:33, 34, and Jeremiah 32:35).

Meaning from Mt. Moriah

This inflexible protection of children had been set into the very core of the life of Israel from their earliest hour when Abraham was interrupted on Mt. Moriah. At that moment he may have been thinking that he would be asked by God to do an act of "worship" identical to the rites of the other religious traditions of his day. After all, he himself had come out of the old Babylonian culture. What Abraham and his son Isaac discovered at Mt. Moriah, however, was the good news that God provides his own sacrifice; our task religiously is to offer the sacrifice of thanksgiving to the Lord of the Lamb for his love for us and to celebrate his love for our sons and daughters (Genesis 22: 12–14).

At Mt. Moriah, in a dramatic way, God once and for all intervened in favor of both the father Abraham and his son Isaac. From then on, the Lord of the Old and New Testaments would continue to stand between father, mother, son, and daughter in order to honor each one. The words to Abraham, "Do not harm the child," are still ringing in our ears. What we must see is that God himself has intervened in a wonderful way in the relationship that we have with our children and with our parents. What we once thought was such a private relationship (and a relationship system), a relationship secretly hidden within the personal boundaries of our own house and our own families, we now see is not so private at all. Jesus Christ is the Mediator in our relationships with our daughters and sons just as he is the Mediator in all other relationships of our lives.

For this reason, St. Paul does not instruct children to obey their parents in any absolute sense; instead he says: "Children, obey your parents *in the Lord*" (Ephesians 6:1). The Lord Jesus Christ is a concerned party in every relationship. Therefore, our obedience toward parents is mediated by the greater authority of Jesus Christ; and that mediation is always in our favor, whether we are child or parent. It means that no one human being, regardless of age or vulnerability, should ever exist in a stark and unprotected interpersonal relationship.

Because of this, we who are people of the Bible have an added Christian stake in the safety of all children. Our Redeemer cares about families and children. We also share this concern for the safety of children with all civilized societies as well. That is the reason that within the laws of most of the states in the United States, any person aware of the abuse of children must report such a situation. We *must* be concerned for the safety of children, who because of their age and their size, cannot protect themselves. "Child abuse" means, quite simply, harm that happens against a child; it may be physical or emotional, but such harm also has spiritual implications as well.

Pastors and professional youth workers, parents, school teachers, and adult volunteers who work with youth must be especially watchful for every instance of the abuse of children. That is why we need to develop skills in the fulfillment of our legal obligations in the defense of "children at risk." But at an even deeper level we must learn positive skills in the healing of those children who have suffered harm and of those adults who cause harm. Our most important task and opportunity lies in the positive encouragement of children whoever they are and whatever they have experienced to this present point in their journey of growing up.

This positive ministry of encouragement of children and adults is what being a friend to the newest one alive is all about. The fact we must realize is how significant the investment in youth is for the very survival and health of civilization itself. But the best part of it all is the reward that is ours and theirs as youth discover their own profound belovedness. It is then that we have shared in the blessing of these members of the population whom Jesus loved so much—the littlest ones alive.

> I wonder how they could hear the shout
> of "I am" when a child
> is born so small?
> But I learned soon that the ones I
> knew very well loved that sound
> of the littlest one to say,
> "It is I."
> Each year there is a surprise for me
> when the someones of my life
> remember my first bold and
> insistent cry
> As the newest one alive.
>
> E.F.P.

-7-

Peace:
The Journey of
Reconciliation

Peace is such a beautiful word. It even sounds good when we hear it spoken: either in Hebrew, *shalom*, arabic *saliim*, or in English, "peace." It is what the world we live in today needs but does not know either how to have or how to keep. The word has profound ethical meanings for the Christian, and it is a key word given by Jesus to his disciples in the Sermon on the Mount.

Jesus Christ began his most famous sermon with a list of nine blessings. One of those reads as follows: "Blessed are the peacemakers, for they shall be called sons of God" (Matthew 5:9). What does it mean to be a "peacemaker" since the word "peace" is a very important word in this text and throughout the Bible? It is first known to us as the Hebrew word *Shalom;* and in the Old Testament this word is used some 250 times. In about twenty-five of those instances, shalom is used as a greeting or farewell. Some fifty to sixty usages of *shalom* carry the meaning of reconciliation such as safety after strife, as for example in 1 Kings 4:25. But in the majority of uses (two-thirds of all instances), *shalom* means fulfillment, wholeness, health, as in Isaiah 54:20. New Testament students know that the Old Testament meanings of words have a most significant linguistic and theological effect upon New Testament words and meanings. Even though the New Testament is written in first century Greek, the thinking and approach to life that undergirds the New

Testament language is more Hebrew than it is Greek. The word "peace" is a good example of this. It is the rich content of *shalom* that decisively influences the appearance and use of the words for peace in the New Testament.

The Many Meanings of "Peace"

One way to test this influence is to note the way that *Shalom* is translated into Greek in the Septuagint, the Greek translation of the Old Testament. According to Jewish tradition this manuscript was written about 100 B.C. by seventy Hebrew rabbis. Because Jewish people involved in tradings and commerce were, as early as that date, already scattering throughout the Mediterranean world, it was necessary for the Jewish community to have a text of the Old Testament written in Greek, the common language of the first century world. In that translation the rabbis used three Greek words to translate the 250 usages of *shalom* in the Old Testament. One word they used was *telios*, which means "fulfillment" and carries the sense of wholeness.

Another word they used was *sazo*, which is the root word for "to save." All of the "salvation" vocabulary of the New Testament therefore has a relationship to the *shalom* vocabulary of the Old Testament. The third word they used is the word *eirene* which carries within it, in classical Greek usage, the sense of "absence of strife," and therefore harmony. But the surest way to understand what this word means is to watch it closely as it is used in each particular setting of Old or New Testament textual sentences. What do we find? We discover three meanings of the words for peace in the Bible:

First, peace is presented in Old and New Testament

texts as a word that derives its force and meaning from a greater source. Like the language of faith, hope, and love, *peace* is a word that gains its full meaning from its source. Peace is a gift that has its origin in God's decision and action. Peace comes from God as in Psalm 29:11. "May the Lord give strength to his people! May the Lord bless his people with peace!"

Second, peace is a word used in both Old and New Testaments to describe the result of God's act in the lives of human beings. It is in this sense that peace and righteousness (justice) cannot be separated. In other words, peace means more to the writers of the Bible than mere absence of conflict. Its meaning is richer; and, therefore, we must use words like "fulfillment" and "health" to really catch the complete meaning of peace in the Bible. Paul has this in mind in 2 Corinthians 13 when he encourages the Corinthians to "live in peace": "Finally, brethren, farewell. Mend your ways, heed my appeal, agree with one another, live in peace, and the God of love and peace will be with you" (2 Corinthians 13:11).

The *third* meaning that emerges from our reading of the uses of the language of peace in the Bible is the active sense of peace as an experience and process of reconciliation. This process takes place in the middle of the real pressures of personal and external turbulence. Our Lord assures his disciples that "In the world you will have tribulation." Nevertheless, there is a peace that he will grant to the disciples in the midst of that pressure of turbulence. It is this powerful peace at work that Jesus describes in John 16:33, "I have said this to you, that in me you may have peace. In the world you have tribulation; but be of good cheer, I have overcome the world."

Here is the peace that reconciles and draws into relationship those who are alienated.

The apostle Paul puts it dramatically when he writes:

> Therefore, since we are justified by faith, we have peace with God through our Lord Jesus Christ (Romans 5:1).

> For if while we were enemies we were reconciled to God by the death of his Son, much more, now that we are reconciled, shall we be saved by his life (Romans 5:10).

We need to reflect upon this third understanding of peace in the Bible in more detail. What is the task and experience of peace as reconciliation? The word *reconcile* in Greek is the root of the English "catalyst." It means an intervention in favor of conflicting parties who are caught up in a warfare so that a new reality of resolution is the result.

Reconciliation as Restraint/Repentance

Reconciliation is a journey that moves through two levels on its way from alienation toward wholeness, from the tearing apart of division to the place of agreement. We need to examine those two parts of the experience of reconciliation so that we may be equipped to play our part as peacemakers in a world deeply alienated spiritually, interpersonally, and internationally.

The first stage in the journey of reconciliation is the experience of restraint/repentance. This first stage describes the slowing down and clearing away of debris so that the next and deeper level of reconciliation may be experienced. When this first intervention stage of the journey happens to us, and upon us by outward action, we call it "restraint." When it happens from within us, we call it "repentance."

Restraint is not peace, but it is an important aspect of the journey toward peace. It is what happens when a boundary appears across the pathway of our lives so that we are compelled to slow down. We have a very decisive example of restraint recorded for us by John in his Gospel:

> They went each to his own house, but Jesus went to the Mount of Olives. Early in the morning he came again to the temple; all the people came to him, and he sat down and taught them. The scribes and the Pharisees brought a woman who had been caught in adultery, and placing her in the midst they said to him, "Teacher, this woman has been caught in the act of adultery. Now in the law Moses commanded us to stone such. What do you say about her?" This they said to test him, that they might have some charge to bring against him. Jesus bent down and wrote with his finger on the ground. And as they continued to ask him, he stood up and said to them, "Let him who is without sin among you be the first to throw a stone at her." And once more he bent down and wrote with his finger on the ground. But when they heard it, they went away, one by one, beginning with the eldest, and Jesus was left alone with the woman standing before him. Jesus looked up and said to her, "Woman, where are they? Has no one condemned you?" She said, "No one, Lord." And Jesus said, "Neither do I condemn you; go and do not sin again" (John 8:1–11).

A woman is caught in the act of adultery and brought by a crowd to Jesus as he taught in Jerusalem. The crowd is apparently prepared to stone this woman and follow the letter of the Law in Leviticus 20:10, even though such a mob action would be in violation of first century Roman law: "If a man commits adultery with the wife of his neighbor, both the adulterer and the adulteress shall be put to death."

The crowd of accusers asks Jesus for his judgment, "What do you say about her?" According to the Gospel-writer John, the crowd is posing the question cynically and for ulterior motives. John informs his readers that they asked him his opinion to tempt him.

Jesus does not answer their question. Instead, he does two things: He bends down to write in the sand; and finally as they continue to put pressure on him to speak, he turns the question toward each of them, "Who of you are sinless. . . ?" Both by what Jesus does and what he says, he restrains the crowd.

First, Jesus bends over and writes on the ground. He slows everything down. He creates a nerve-wracking, kingly silence. This is restraint. His words to the crowd also become a barrier or boundary for those who thought they were ready to stone their prisoner to death. "From the eldest to the youngest they went away." This is restraint; it is not resolution; it is not salvation, but it is the essential first step before a resolution can happen. It is a boundary that protects the people from doing more harm than has already been done. Already the crowd has tempted Jesus, and now will they add to that sin murder?

Jesus placed himself as that barrier across the pathway of cumulating violence. This sort of restraint happens in our century when alarmed neighbors rush out into the hallway of a dorm to stop a fight that breaks out between two students. It is the role that a peace officer plays in attempting to stop a crime in progress. It is the role of the multinational, peace-keeping, military presence in a country like Nambia.

We cannot describe this restraint as a lasting solution to the very complicated mixture of ancient and recent suspicion, injustice and fear that is present in the various population groups and nations of southwest Africa, or any other social situation; but the restraint of a ceasefire or a truce is, nevertheless, a necessary part of the whole journey.

Restraint, therefore, is the intervention that happens from forces outside our lives so that a slowing down happens. This slowing down should never be confused with the peace that is the wholeness of health and resolution. Certainly, however, it is better than the violence that only compounds the damage already done.

Restraint in a Riot

The ways that restraint takes place are sometimes incongruous and even humorous. I remember a riot in Berkeley during the spring of 1972. A car had been overturned by the rioters just in front of our church at the corner of Dana Street and Channing Way. Two Berkeley firemen were attempting to spray foam over the spilling gasoline when a crowd began to jeer them, and several people began throwing rocks at them. I was very upset by the whole event when in front of me a young man took up a rock to throw. Suddenly, and with my most authoritative voice, I said to him, "What are you doing with that rock? I'm the pastor of this church, and that rock is church property. You're not going to throw that rock because it belongs to First Presbyterian Church. So, put it down."

The young man looked at me and laughed and threw the rock down as I had told him to. He walked away and said cheerfully to me, "I used to be a pacifist too. . . ."

Actually, I wasn't so much a classical philosophical pacifist in that situation; but I was a restrainer, at least in this case. He had been temporarily protected by my command from the cowardly act he was just about to commit with one of our rocks. There was no time to grapple with the deeper intellectual, political, religious issues, and feelings of rage or fear or even boredom that brought him to where he was on that afternoon; but at least one barrier had forced him to slow down and hesitate, let alone the fact that my command provided a possible protection of a fireman trying to prevent the disaster of a gasoline fire.

The restraint that happens from within us is what the Bible calls *repentance*. There are several other ingredients also present in the human experience of repentance, but one of the most important elements in repentance is what might be described as self-restraint. It means that we ourselves realize the harm happening to us and through us so that we make the decision to stop and look for another step toward peace.

The prodigal son "comes to himself" and decides to find his way back to his father. He does not suddenly have peace by this decision of repentance with its moral spiritual ingredient of admission of guilt on his part. But he does turn toward the relationship where the surprise of resolution and healing and peace will unexpectedly become his experience, because of the amazing grace of his waiting father.

We live in a world that needs to discover the good

effects of this early and tentative stage of the reconciliation journey. It is the first step toward a more substantial total possibility of resolution. In an essay in the book *From Under the Rubble* Alexander Solzhenitzyn has called upon the great nations of the world to embrace this value. He calls it the "old Christian" value of self-restraint. His argument is both powerful and timely:

> After repentance, comes self-limitation. Repentance creates the atmosphere for self-limitation. Self-limitation on the part of individuals has often been observed and described, and it is well-known to all of us; but as far as I know, no state has ever carried through a deliberate policy of self-limitation or set itself such a task in general form. Though when it has done so at difficult moments in some particular sector, such as food rationing or fuel rationing, then self-limitation has paid off handsomely.

Restraints, both from within or without, are not in themselves peace; but what they do offer to us is time and opportunity. A truce is not a just treaty, but it does offer breathing space, time for thinking and room for negotiating. This time to think and repent is what Jesus provides to the crowd in Jerusalem and also to the accused woman when he asks, "Where are your accusers?"

"They have all left, Lord," she replies.

"Neither do I accuse you, go and sin no more," Jesus concludes. He has interposed his own person and authority into an angry and volatile incident, and a gift that he has given both to the mob and to one lonely, accused, human being is the gift of time. It is time to think, to wonder, to repent, to decide.

According to John, the very next words that our Lord spoke on the way of righteousness are these words, "Again Jesus spoke to them, saying, 'I am the light of the world; he who follows me will not walk in darkness, but will have the light of life'" (John 8:12). In God's design the experience of restraint is intended to be one part of the longer journey that leads to righteousness. We who live under God's grace are grateful for this restraint, and we see it as one more sign of God's grace. We do not glorify this time and opportunity as if it were more significant than it is, but we are grateful for it; and we should work hard for it in the present threats to peace situations of our generation so that the greater goals of *shalom* may be realized.

There needs to be the restraint of civilization and of the organization of people in the social contract so that human beings can be as close to each other as possible without doing harm to one another. As Christians we eagerly work for the fullest possibilities of relationship with people because we have the good news of God's peace to share with our neighbors. Since the coming of God's peace we have all the more reason to work hard for the temporary ceasefires and truce agreements that allow for time and relationship-building. This is a strong argument in favor of Christians who plan careers in such professions as law enforcement and politics.

As I see it, this is one of the major moral flaws in blood revolution or the bloody suppression of the threats of insurgency, because after such runaway vengeance and when it is finally all quiet on the western or eastern front, we discover in grief that people have died who might have been reconciled. Now there is no longer time for that. It is the gray light of despair that follows the red blood of revolution and this is why we must be very careful about the glorification of revolution.

Peace That Lasts

What is peace at the deeper level? Let us now return to first principles. The Lord who gave to us the peace-making mandate has also given us the whole peace to go with it. The peace that lasts is a fourfold peace that restores relationship toward God, toward myself, toward my neighbor, and toward the earth. It is the peace that results in righteousness. This peace takes time to build because it is a dynamic and not a static reality. It is the peace we submit to in faith as we trust in Jesus Christ to be our Savior and to grant his peace to us. This ministry of peace-making happens as ordinary Christians with the equipment of the gospel stay close to where people really live and study and work. If you are planning your future career, why not give yourself to a peace-making career at some place along the vital continuum we have been discovering?

One of my favorite scenes in the children's stories of C. S. Lewis, The Chronicles of Narnia, takes place in *The Lion, the Witch and the Wardrobe* just following the great victory of Aslan over the witch at the stone table. Lucy and Susan are invited to join Aslan and while on his great back run throughout the land, setting free those in Narnia who had been turned to stone during the oppressive reign of Jadis the winter witch. Before they could ride on Aslan's back, however, it was necessary for the Great Lion himself to become their peace and heal the treachery of Edmund their brother. Aslan not only resolved the treachery of sin, he also healed the fears of each of the sons and the daughters of Adam. We cannot do the work of peace-making until there is first peace in our own lives. In the divine logic of biblical ethics we are not commanded to *share* love until we first *experience* love: "Beloved, let us love one another" (1 John 4:7). So it is with peace. Jesus said: "I have said this to you, that in me you may have peace. In the world you have tribulation; but be of good cheer, I have overcome the world."

-8-

Choose Life

Jesus once told a parable about himself as the shepherd. In that parable he made one of his most unforgettable promises: "I have come that you might have life and have it more abundantly" (John 10:10). Jesus Christ as the Good Shepherd makes that promise. While it is not above the promise of the eternal life of salvation, the context of John 10 (and other places in the New Testament as well) makes one thing clear. Jesus as the Lord of life calls his followers to experience the full benefit of its living wholeness here and now in the place where we are now alive and breathing!

Throughout the Bible there is a hearty celebration of life that shows itself at the time of marriage and at the time of birth. Hannah sings a song because of the birth of a child just as Mary the mother of our Lord will sing a song when she hears the prophecy of her own pregnancy. Throughout the Bible we have been granted a preference for life, an encouragement to celebrate life and a respect for life deeply rooted in the Law and the Gospel.

The breath and the blood of all living beings are honored in Jewish law because they are recognized as the signs of life. For us, therefore, one of the great nonnegotiable markers that gives direction along the pathway of our own life journey is this endorsement of the life signpost. It is a reminder to us of the importance of our own existence. It is also a mandate that calls us to choose life over death, to preserve life against all that harms and destroys, and to enrich life with the abundance that Jesus invited us to experience.

Look closely at the sixth commandment. It states this signpost in a grand and good negative sentence that echoes in our minds whenever we think about life and the lives of others.

"You shall not kill" (Exodus 20:13). The word translated "kill" in the English text is the Hebrew *rasah*, which means "anti-social killing" (von Rad, p. 59). It is most accurately translated by the English word "Murder." The word is used forty-six times in the Old Testament, and, as Brevard Childs points out in his study, the largest number of usages carry the intent of the taking of life in the context of blood vengeance, in which the act of murder occurs because of hatred and malice.

Commanded Not to Cross Over

The sixth commandment denies the right of any person among us to take into his or her own hands with a harmful intent the life of another person. We are commanded not to cross over another person's right to live. This brief mandate is greatly expanded in the code or "ordinances" (RSV) of the law within the books of Moses, and from that expansion the restraint takes shape in several directions. Within the expansion it becomes clear that because of this commandment, individuals in society are not allowed to take vengeance against those who have done harm; it is only the community that shall take action against the wrongdoers. The right of capital punishment is preserved strictly for the community. The code also makes it clear that the community must exercise this right only after the verification of wrongdoing through hearings and by attestation of witnesses (Leviticus 19:20, Exodus 21:22; 23:3). The community must make its judgments according to the provisions in the Law and ordinances which become a safeguard against impetuous and informal punishment of wrongdoers. This commandment takes away from the individual the right either to initiate harm or to "even the score" when harm takes place. Both of these kinds of violence, murder and vengeance, are implied in the word *rasah*. The Law offers to us a four-word (in English) command against such violence.

The expansion of the Law in the ordinances also makes it clear that the commandment is not qualified as to the designation of those protected by the command. This, like all of the Torah, is a universal commandment. The principle of equal justice under law becomes a basic ingredient in the ordinances. "You shall do no injustice in judgment; you shall not be partial to the poor or defer to the great, but in righteousness shall you judge your neighbor" (Leviticus 19:15). This equality under the law is also affirmed for the foreigner. "When a stranger sojourns with you in your land, you shall not do him wrong. . . . For you were strangers in the land of Egypt" (Leviticus 19:33, 34).

The restraint guaranteed in the principle of equal justice under law and equal justice for all sets apart the Jewish law from the codes of neighboring civilizations of the same period. The difference becomes clear when the Jewish Torah is contrasted to the Code of Hammurabi (Babylonian): "If a man strike a gentleman's daughter that she dies, his own daughter is to be put to death, if a poor man's, the slayer pays one half mina." In the law of the books of Moses, we each pay for our own crimes and the justice is prescribed equally.

In this context we can better appreciate the purpose of the technical nature of the code as it attempts to find proper equations. On the one hand, the justice handed out by the community honors the harmed person by being equivalent to the loss. On the other, the punishments do not spiral in intensity beyond that principle of even exchange. One of the most famous verses of the Old Testament is a sentence from the ordinances that seeks to achieve this just and middle position: "If any harm follows, then you shall give life for life, eye for eye, tooth for tooth, hand for hand, foot for foot, burn for burn, wound for wound, stripe for stripe" (Exodus 21:23–25). This sentence is not so much a description of punishment as it is a limit upon runaway revenge that the community may demand from a wrongdoer.

Stated Negatively, Meant Positively

Though the sixth commandment is stated in broad negative terms, the intention of the Law is positive. It is a commandment in favor of life. Because human life is so meaningful in the sight of God, we are not to take human life into our hands with a harmful intent. The strong word *rasah* makes it clear that this commandment is not correctly interpreted as a command against the slaughter of animals for food. *Rasah* carried within it the intent of malice, the kind of malice experienced within human relationships and estrangement. But once the Law has made the protection of life from harm its focus, we are drawn by the commandment to embrace the Law's positive implication. This deeper level is expressed in Leviticus 19:17–18:

"You shall not hate your brother in your heart, but you shall reason with your neighbor, lest you bear sin because of him. You shall not take vengeance or bear any grudge against the sons of your own people, but you shall love your neighbor as yourself: I am the Lord."

We are not only to restrain ourselves from doing harm. We are also creatively to do good toward our neighbor. It is this latter direction that Jesus impresses upon the Leviticus text with the parable of the good Samaritan in Luke 10. The issue is not the method of determining a correct definition of the neighbor who deserves my care but, rather, the word neighbor is seen in the eyes of Jesus as positive and dynamic: "Who proved neighbor to the man who fell among the robbers?"

The apostle Paul also draws the sixth commandment out to this logical conclusion in his Letter to the Romans:

> Owe no one anything except to love one another; for he who loves his neighbor has fulfilled the law. The commandments, "You shall not commit adultery, You shall not kill, You shall not steal, You shall not covet," and any other commandment, are summed up in this sentence, "You shall love your neighbor as yourself." Love does no wrong to a neighbor; therefore love is the fulfilling of the law (13:8–10).

God's holy will in favor of life is the larger context within which the sixth commandment states its protection of life from the murderer. Therefore, this good side of the sixth commandment is the greater mandate: How can I enrich and deepen the quality of life around me, not only my own, but the life of my neighbor? In the language of the gospel, the mandate is even bolder. How can I bring new life to those who have lost hope of life? This is a convictional value worth living for. It is a signpost that shows me the way to go.

There are complex ethical questions that properly relate to the sixth commandment, and we must now try to put those issues into a whole biblical perspective. They concern questions of suicide, abortion, euthanasia, capital punishment, and war. The big questions for me in the midst of my journey are these: What am I to do regarding issues like these? How do I act when I am faced with them?

Suicide—the Murder of Self

Suicide is now the number one cause of death among youth in America. Each one of us needs help in the face of this present crisis of meaning in life. By the sixth commandment we are denied the right of vengeance, which belongs to God alone. This means that we as human beings do not have the authority or the right to pronounce the last word on any human being—others or ourselves. Suicide is an act of violence by which a person arrogantly takes the right of judgment into his or her own hands. It is vengeance against oneself. The reasons in each separate instance are usually very complicated. In many situations the ability to reason may be clouded or totally confused because of despair, substance abuse, or physical illness. The sixth commandment offers no rules of exception, and therefore suicide is against the will of God in the perspective of the Law.

Because it is the murder of the self, it involves the destruction of relationships. Suicide is also a self-decision against the will of God as revealed to us in the gospel. It is the violent rejection of hope and belovedness toward the human self. Suicide is distrust of the faithfulness of God and his imprint of meaning upon life. Thus it is a violent act against the meaning of all of life. That is one of the reasons why this act has such a devastating effect upon the members of the family and the friends who are abandoned by this violence.

G. K. Chesterton put it this way: "Suicide . . . is the refusal to take an interest in existence. . . . The man who kills a man, kills a man. The man who kills himself, kills all men. . . . The thief compliments the things he steals, if not the owner of them. But the suicide insults everything on earth by not stealing it" (*Orthodoxy*, pp. 72–73).

Can Death Be "Good"?

Euthanasia, like suicide, seeks the solution to the problems of life through death. The word euthanasia—"good death"—promises that there can be a good death, but the death we bring on ourselves for any reason is not a good death. Death is a foe, an enemy, the spoiler of our stewardship and relationships on earth. What we are promised in biblical faith is the victory over death, not the embrace of death. Paul quotes this deep longing of the prophets Isaiah and Hosea in his affirmation of this theology:

> For this perishable nature must put on the imperishable, and this mortal nature must put on immortality. When the perishable puts on the imperishable, and the mortal puts on immortality, then shall come to pass the saying that is written:

113

"Death is swallowed up in victory."
"O death, where is thy victory?
O death, where is thy sting?"
The sting of death is sin, and the power of sin is the law.
But thanks be to God, who gives us the victory through
our Lord Jesus Christ (1 Corinthians 15:53–57).

The biblical road markers of the Law and the
Prophets warn each of us against euthanasia which is
assuming the right to decide against the continuing life
of another human being on the basis of our own judgment. In effect, we decide what constitutes meaningful
quality of life for another human being. This is the warning against the destruction of life because we have determined, on the basis of our own usefulness or quality of
life scale, that another person's interests are served best
by a "good death" rather than a hard life.

This warning against euthanasia does not mean,
however, that human death, which is the natural conclusion of every human journey, should be artificially pro-
longed by medical technology. The present capabilities of
medical care have made available to us skills sufficient to
radically intervene at times of grave physical crisis.
There are now medical-technical interventions capable of
artificially sustaining the human body functions of respi-
ration, cardiac activity, and bodily nourishment. These
radical interventions are an exciting part of the stewardship of medicine, and we are grateful for their intervention at times of an assault of injury or illness against the
human body. This does not mean, however, that these
extreme medical interventions are warranted when their
use is no longer a means of possible cure but, instead, the
extension of the process of dying.

The grand positive value of the sixth commandment is our mandate to favor life. That positive imperative inspires us to fight hard to save every life when it is threatened by the violence of injury, illness, or any other threat. However, this grand positive that embraces life is also able to accept death, knowing that the gift of eternal life through Jesus Christ is a greater gift and of greater power than any human death. Death is not good, but it is not the final word on our existence. Therefore, when we must in humility finally accept our own death and the death of other people whom we cherish in this life, that acceptance is itself surrounded by hope just as it is surrounded by love.

A Look at Abortion

Abortion which terminates an unwanted pregnancy is a violent act against a separate life. The moral arrogance of abortion rests in the argument that because a life is unwanted, it therefore ceases to have worth or deserve protection. But this argument is repudiated in the Law and the gospel. In the Bible the orphan and the widow are especially singled out for protection (Exodus 22:21–24). In the New Testament, because of the healing power of the gospel, even the enemy is protected from my anger (Romans 12:19–21). Abortion treats the unborn child as our enemy. But the unborn is not our enemy; rather, it is our life. Because of the worth of each separate life, the medical and personal decision concerning the possibility of abortion must be a very hard decision. It is never a good decision, even though it may be the right decision among hard choices in that instance when the life of the mother who is now present with us is endangered by pregnancy. It then becomes the right moral stewardship of life to choose the life of the person who is with us in present relationship over the life that is only potentially with us.

When abortion is a necessary choice, then the biblically established checks and balances of community participation in that decision are essential. The principle of the sixth commandment in the expansion of the Law (Deuteronomy, Leviticus) is that no one person acting alone has the right to take life away. This is the reasoning for the Old Testament tradition of community due process of law with protection safeguards established in favor of the accused. From this standpoint it can never be argued that the abortion decision is to be made by a woman alone, as if it were only her decision.

An unborn child is a separate life from the life of his or her mother and father. A child born or unborn is not spiritually or biologically a part of the body, either of a mother or a father. This is the logic that protects children from abusive parents.

The community at large has a profound interest and concern in what happens to children within the privacy of their homes. Therefore, strict laws that safeguard those who cannot protect themselves are both right and wise in a civilized society. Every abortion decision must be the hard choice of not only a woman who experiences a problem pregnancy but also of her community. This system of balances happens through safeguard measures established by the community to protect the potential life from hasty decisions.

We who trust God have a vital concern to share with our society in this matter—as in every case where the meaning of life is at stake. Our role is to share and work toward a more humane understanding of human life. This understanding of the value of human life is one of the gifts we have to give our culture as thoughtfully and wisely as is possible—even when the culture of which we are a part is unwilling or for some reason unable to hear our concerns. We need to share our respect for human life in a holistic way, first of all by the ways we model the worth of life and care about human beings. We also need to express our advocacy about such issues as abortion with skill and with reasons.

It is decidedly not helpful when the stewardship of birth control through the prevention of pregnancy is confused with the question of abortion. Throughout biblical faith and life, we as God's people have been mandated by God to care thoughtfully for the earth and to plan carefully for our family. We must be able to care properly for our children in their growing-up years, physically and educationally. They need to be free to grow in knowledge and righteousness. This command to steward life upon the earth is a mandate that calls upon human families to make responsible choices. The size of a family is one of those proper stewardship choices that I must not escape, either through ignorance about consequences or by irresponsible acts on my part. I cannot ask for God's blessing upon my own refusal to make ethical stewardship decisions.

The right of capital punishment is allowed to the community in the Law's expansion through the ordinances of Exodus and Leviticus (for example, Exodus 22:12–17). The death penalty is prescribed as a punishment for grave wrongdoing, but it is to be executed only by the community. In the same way war is a community action determined by community policy. In both instances the community has made the determination that a person or nation or group is an enemy that must be opposed.

Can War Be "Just"?

The concept of just war has been broadly discussed and argued throughout the history of Old and New Testament theology. The issue is not simple; because of the reality of human sinfulness at the local community level, it is necessary that law enforcement officers be armed and prepared to take violent action against those who endanger the lives of others. The problem of war is that same crisis, but it is extended to the international level. Martin Luther attempted to draw together the implications of the total biblical witness to develop a perspective on the issue:

> For what is just war but the punishment of evil doers and the maintenance of peace? . . . take my advice, dear Lords. Stay out of war unless you have to defend and protect yourselves and your office compels you to fight . . . [Luther gives bold advice to his parishioners concerning the call to war that is unjust.] "Suppose my Lord were wrong in going to war." I reply: If you know for sure that he is wrong, then you should neither fight nor serve, for you cannot have a good conscience before God (*Writings*, pp. 438–70).

But the larger question of the determination of the community's correct stance toward an enemy has been permanently altered for the biblical Christian because of

the way in which Jesus Christ fulfilled the commandments and covenants and yearnings of the Old Testament.
Jesus Christ has taken the place of the sinner; this is the
meaning of the cross. Therefore, all the punishments prescribed in the code converge toward and into this one
man, who has "canceled the bond which stood against us
with its legal demands; this he set aside, nailing it to the
cross" (Colossians 2:14). Because of this event on Good
Friday and Easter we who trust in Jesus Christ as Savior-
Lord must see other human beings in the perspective of
their belovedness. They may not know of that belovedness, but we who have ourselves discovered God's love
do, and that makes all the difference to us.

This viewpoint deeply influences how we must interpret the angry provisions of the code as well as the angry
psalms in which the psalmist is praying for the destruction of an enemy. We know that Jesus Christ himself has
taken the place of that enemy. Therefore, those texts must
be read in the light of their fulfillment. Jesus has identified himself with the sinner. That is good news for us
because we are sinners. Now that good news is also an
ethical challenge to us because there are sinners all
around us. This redeeming identification of Jesus Christ
creates both a positive and a restraining effect.

At this point in our consideration of the sixth commandment we need to look closely at the restraining
influence of this "holy interruption" of both the commandment and the Lord of that commandment. The restraining impact of our Lord's identification with the
enemy, the sinner, is dramatically portrayed to us by an
incident recorded in John's Gospel (John 8:1–11). Here
the question of capital punishment is plainly put to Jesus

by a group of Pharisees and Sadducees (see E. F. Palmer's discussion in *The Intimate Gospel: Studies in John,* pp. 83–87). In this incident Jesus places his own life between the crowd and the accused woman caught in the act of adultery. As he writes in the sand he slows down the total event and makes himself the central object of focus. "What do you say about her?" The crowd shouts out to him. But Jesus turns the question toward the accusers: "Let him who is without sin among you be the first to throw a stone."

Jesus has done a remarkable thing. He has restrained a crowd from doing more harm than they have already done. According to John they had brought the accused person to Jesus not because of concern for the preservation of marriage, but in order to tempt Jesus. This means that the crowd is already guilty of tempting the Lord. But Jesus protects the crowd from adding to that transgression the sin of unjust vengeance. He has also refocused the event both toward himself and toward ourselves. He protects the crowd and the woman, but because of this bold act in favor of this one human being and the angry crowd the shadow of the cross is over this intervention.

A new refocusing is produced for us not only by the incident of John 8 but also by the central incident of all time, the cross and empty tomb. Because of this refocusing, the Christian interpreter of the angry tests of the Old Testament cannot see them apart from their fulfillment. Jesus Christ has absorbed the anger of David's psalms of hate as much as he has fulfilled the greatness of David's psalms of hope. Because of the authority of the Redeemer, we are therefore restrained. And because of the powerful love of the Redeemer we are able to offer a new strategy in the face of the ancient vicious cycle of hatred between enemies.

The restraint element present in the Law and deepened by the gospel of Jesus Christ makes me personally very uneasy about the practice of capital punishment by modern societies. The problem morally is that when a criminal has been caught and is then completely at our mercy, that criminal is no longer a threat to the community. Execution of the condemned has only the purpose of extreme, irrevocable, and final public punishment. From a pastoral standpoint, I am also concerned at the impact capital punishment has upon those who practice it. It harms the community because the community takes too much interest in it. We want to see evil-doers punished, and that desire has a harmful and dehumanizing effect upon the people in the community.

In the case of murder, it seems to me that the principal human equation shattered by the violent criminal should be repaid by the criminal through a life sentence without possibility of parole. The criminal should spend those years in hard labor to repay the injured parties and society. The celebrity status of the isolated "death row" prisoners is not meaningful punishment. There are also implications of this that reach out toward the institution of prisons. Because life is so precious, those who harm life cannot be excused by human warehouse-like imprisonment. They need some spiritual-moral journey possibility of which work and obligation to repay are essential ingredients.

War is always a bad choice, though military confrontation is sometimes the lesser of bad choices. The counsel of self-restraint which becomes the dominant thread of the sixth through the tenth commandments is the needed ingredient in the twentieth century face-off between nations. It is the first step toward reconciliation. The slow-down of the possibilities of violence made possible by that restraint provides time for the emergence of greater positive realities. The spirit of the Law is that before we act precipitously, we should stop and listen to God; we should learn and then act.

"Thou shalt not kill" is a good restraint. It is a law in our favor that alerts us to the high value God places upon human life. It becomes one more sign along the road of how much we mean to the Lord of the Law. Restraint is one more mark of our worth that has its origins in both the Law and the gospel.

Alexander Solzhenitsyn argues for self-limitation between nations as an essential first step toward world peace. "After repentance, and once we renounce the use of force, self-limitation comes into its own as the most natural principle to live by. Repentance creates the atmosphere for self-limitation . . . the idea of self-limitation in society is not a new one. We find it a century ago in such thoroughgoing Christians as the Russian old believers" (*From Under the Rubble*, pp. 135–136).

-9-

Keep Your Promises

Human beings *make* promises and *hear* promises. Therefore, we welcome a signpost that reminds each of us who travel together on the roadway to keep the promises we make. This is the sort of mandate that always makes good sense to us, whether we follow the advice or not. We *want* to be able to trust in the promises we hear. There are promises we make to one another which become our commitments, and promises we make to God which are the human part of the equation called faith. Of all the promises we make to the people in our lives, none are as important and have as far-reaching consequences as the commitments between a man and a woman that create a marriage relationship. The seventh commandment has to do with the promises we make in marriage. We need to carefully examine and understand this very simple imperative because, though the command is deceptively brief, its implications for all promises are far reaching when the law is seen in the larger context of its grand, positive intention of God.

"You shall not commit adultery" (Exodus 20:14). The Deuteronomomic text linguistically unites the sixth through the tenth commandment of the law into a single fabric by repeating the word "neither." "You shall not kill. *Neither* shall you commit adultery. *Neither* shall you steal. *Neither* shall you bear false witness against your neighbor. *Neither* shall you covet your neighbor's house, his field, or his manservant, or his maidservant, his ox, or his ass, or anything that is your neighbor's" (Deuteronomy 5:17–21, italics mine).

The effect of this textual unity is to draw together the seventh, eighth, ninth, and tenth commandments and place them within the larger framework of the sixth. This shows that the reverence for life which undergirds the sixth command is now carried forth into other interpersonal and social ethical directions. There is, therefore, a connection in the perspective of the Torah between the kind of disloyal hurtfulness involved in adultery or false witness and the destructive hurtfulness involved in the merciless vengeance of murder.

Also, the grand, positive element in the sixth commandment, which honors life and respects the life space of the neighbor who lives alongside of me, becomes the positive motivational context for such commands as the imperative concerning marriage, telling the truth, etc. Marriage is where the word "commitment" means the most in human relationships. Therefore the Ten Commandments are wise first to focus upon marriage when the whole understanding of interpersonal commitments is intended.

Adultery

The word, "adultery," as it is used throughout the Bible, describes the unfaithfulness of married persons. "It is clear from the evidence that throughout the O.T. adultery was placed in a different category from fornication" (Childs, p. 422). At its deepest level this commandment has to do with marriage and its importance in

God's sight. It is not a commandment about sexual sins in general, or about youthful morality, though there is an inevitable relationship between marriage and all interpersonal morality.

Two different kinds of sin are at work in sexual immorality in general, and adultery in particular. One is a hot sin, and the other is a cold sin. Fornication, sexual sin between the unmarried, is a hot sin and must be treated as such. Serious dangers are involved in the carelessness and lack of concern for another human being that goes with this transgression. Fornication is warned against in Deuteronomy and in New Testament teaching as well (note Exodus 22:16–17, Deuteronomy 22:28–29, 1 Corinthians 7:36).

From the biblical point of view, no sin is more devastating than the act of adultery. Adultery breaks a commitment that has been made between two people and destroys a relationship and a family. Far-reaching destructive results are the consequence of adultery in the life of all those persons who are related to that family. In my view, however, C. S. Lewis is correct in describing most instances of adultery as cold sins. His nefarious senior devil Screwtape makes this observation:

> Then there was the lukewarm casserole of adulterers. Could you find in it any trace of a fully inflamed, defiant, rebellious, insatiable lust? I couldn't. They all tasted to me like undersexed morons who had blundered or trickled into the wrong beds in automatic response to sexy advertisements, or to make themselves feel modern and emancipated, or . . . even because they had nothing else to do (*The Screwtape Letters,* p. 155).

Adultery is the sin of abandonment, of loss of interest, of rejection, of self-pity. Most adultery is not at all like the highly charged carelessness of the young who have strong feelings and because of those feelings they are carried away with their desire for another person. Instead, adultery is too often the desperate act of those who have gone stale in the afternoon of their lives and are feeling sorry for themselves because they think they are unhappy. They have no energy left to work hard on the adult relationship called marriage. Out of this exhaustion most people drift into adultery.

Dorothy L. Sayers has noted the same thing: "What commonly happens in periods of disillusionment . . . when philosophies are bankrupt and life appears without hope—men and women may turn to lust in sheer boredom and discontent, trying to find in it some stimulus" (*Christian Letters to a Post-christian World,* p. 139).

The seventh commandment uses strong and negative language to warn against the sin of adultery, but underneath this negative mandate, like a foundation stone, stands the positive affirmation concerning marriage. The point is this: the central concern of the Law and the gospel is not the "negative" achievement of a man and wife who have never been unfaithful to each other, but rather it is the positive health of their life together that is at the heart of the grand design. More important than not committing adultery is to share love and commitment toward each other.

Something More Than Faithfulness

Sometimes in a pastoral counseling situation a man or woman will say to me, "I have never been unfaithful to my spouse." This is one good and important building block, but it is not enough of a foundation to build a warm and nourishing home. The question I want to ask such a person is this: "But what have you done positively to grow in your faithfulness together?"

It is not enough to stand before God and humanity and say, "I have never murdered anyone." This negative achievement is commendable but hardly adequate to satisfy the grand intention of God's law. Have you loved "your neighbor as yourself" (Leviticus 19:18)? Have you "proved neighbor to the man who fell among the robbers" (Luke 10)? In the same way the family needs more than mere faithfulness to fulfill the mandate's intention, but it does need faithfulness!

The larger question has to do with the creative nourishment and growth of the privilege of life together called marriage. The law has provided a critical boundary line. But in this case, as with the other ethical commandments, it is a minimal standard. From it, two people work toward the joy and the loving interpersonal relationship that make marriage what it must be in order to stand at its post of vital importance in the whole journey of human life.

Marriage thrives when the partners in the relationship have forgotten how to keep score at the minimal boundary lines of the Law's requirement, because marriage for them is a maximum relationship. It happens when a man and woman are more excited about the road they travel together than the false side ways and dead-end streets they avoided. The intent of the commandment is positive faithfulness, which is the source of the most joyous and liberating possibilities in human relationship.

Freedom between two human beings is then the exciting result of this positive commitment.

Commitments and promises have a wider purpose than their importance to the interpersonal bonding of marriage, however. We make many promises every day as part of our daily participation in life. There are promises that we make in our work and promises we make with the wholeness of our lives which become discipleship commandments and missional promises.

We use the English word, "professional," to refer to certain categories of workers. We describe a doctor and a lawyer as a professional man or woman. The word comes from a Latin root that means "promise." This means that a doctor has made a promise to his or her patients, just as a lawyer makes a promise to both client and court.

We cannot survive as a civilized people without promises and people who keep the promises they make. Nevertheless, there are people who have great difficulty in making promises. These are often not persons who are unfaithful in keeping promises. Rather, their problem is that they dare not promise even when the evidence in favor of commitment is clear and adequate. These are the ones who have a problem of fearfulness toward decision making. The result in their lives is a learned pattern of hesitation and withdrawal from moments of promising.

Daily life needs decisions to make the separate parts of our deepest hopes and our loves and our practical purposes come together and become a realized wholeness. We can feel an infatuation for a person that may develop into genuine romance. However, without the promise, without a personal commitment at some definite moment, the relationship will fade away as all infatuations finally do.

The grand positive of the seventh commandment is this: "Thou shalt make a commitment that you keep." The commandment does not assume that every person must be in a married state to be a complete person, but it does encourage the men and women who love another person to dare to make a lifelong promise to that person.

Wisdom is a skill that frees me up just enough to make promises. Then long-term integrity takes over and I decide to keep the promises I have dared to make.

-10-

Property Value and
Human Value

Things are more important to us than we are ever willing to admit. Thus the right to own property has always been a highly protected and defended human value. We get a very sick feeling in our stomach when we discover that someone has stolen something from us. Why is this so? It is because we sense a profoundly ominous invasion of our right to exist. The theft of our property is like the first stage of the theft of our lives. Intuitively we realize that if the things in my hand are not safely mine to have and hold without the danger of robbery, then how safe is my hand itself? Is not the theft of my property just the first stage of the destruction of my life?

It doesn't make it any easier if there are religious or socio-political reasons for the theft either! Naboth owned some valuable land that King Ahab and the king's ambitious wife, Jezebel, wanted very much to have. With religious and political treachery the king's wife managed to steal this land. Then she saw to it that Naboth was destroyed too. We feel the horror of this connection between property and life as the narrative of this brutal theft of property and life is told in the Old Testament Book of 1 Kings.

Boris Pasternak recounts the same kind of loss of dignity in his telling of the political theft of Yuri Androvich's house in Moscow by a committee of comrades who progressively take from Dr. Zhivago everything distinctly his. Finally they take *him!* The reasons in 1917 are spoken in the revolutionary language of communist collectivization and ownership of the people, but the dehumanizing result is the same.

Jesus of Nazareth does not ask for the property of his followers. Proof of this is demonstrated in one instance to a wealthy young man in which Jesus suggests that the man sell what he has, *give it to the poor,* and then follow Jesus. Jesus Christ does not say to this young prospective disciple, "Sell what you have and bring your money to me and follow. . . ." The whole point of this encounter is that wealth should be carefully stewarded for good use by the young man himself. He has this responsibility as a part of his life in virtue of the fact that wealth has been entrusted to him.

We know that theft is wrong in the Bible whether by the king with political reasons or by priests with religious reasons—or by ordinary folk for any reasons. "Thou shalt not steal" is the eighth commandment.

Persons and Possessions

But why is this value important in a positive sense? The connection between the human personality and the possession of houses and land is significant theologically. It gives a double clue within the Law and the gospel that human beings are not regarded by God as disembodied spirits. Men and women in the Bible are perceived in concrete terms and are never spiritualized. The human being is always seen in the Old and New Testaments as a real person in a real place who wears a certain distinctive clothing, lives at a particular address, and has special relationships that go with the concreteness that our possessions represent. The names in the Bible emphasize this particularly: Simon son of John, Judas from Kerioth, James the short one, Thomas the twin. The view of persons in the eighth commandment is in the sharpest contrast possible to that of the late first century Gnostics, who held a totally spiritualized vision of the ideal of man and woman. By contrast, the Judeo-Christian vision of persons is concrete and specific. Therefore the hope for the future contains this same concreteness at its core— not the absorption of the soul into cosmic immortality, but the resurrection of the body. It is the whole self that has meaning in the present, and the whole self is destined toward hope as well.

This concrete view of persons is imprinted into the Torah from its opening preface, which reminds Israel of the actual physical, political, and social rescue from Egypt. The concreteness is preserved throughout the mandates of the Law. All the narratives of the life of the people in the Old and New Testaments in different ways make it clear that God's will for life has to do with the real lives of real people here and now. From this standpoint we can understand why the biblical messianic expectation of the prophets and the psalmists demands a Redeemer who shares with us in our real lives. A "phantom Christ," who is so spiritual that he is not fully human, can never be the fulfillment of the people of the Ten Commandments. He must be "born of woman, born under the law" (Galatians 4:4).

In the same way, a political vision for social life which disregards the need of a human being to have real property and real place is a political vision that does not understand human personhood. Nor does that vision treasure human personhood, either. A person needs concreteness just as a person needs ideas.

"Thou shalt not steal" affirms the individuality of persons, but this commandment also warns against the idolatry of concreteness. The greedy fascination with any part of the created order that causes a person to steal is portrayed as a temptation to sin; it is against the will of God to seize possessions or relationships that belong to other people. Instead, we are mandated to respect a preserved distance between our own ambitions and the life space of other human beings around us.

If the positive intention of this commandment is followed to its ultimate goal, the result in human personality is very healthy. It means that in our encounters with other people, we are to recognize their concreteness and their right to exist within a preserved space. Once we are set free from the temptation to steal, we may then relate to other people for *who* they are and not for *what* they own.

The Privilege of Property

It is ironic that when we trust the intention of the eighth commandment toward the privilege of property, both for our neighbor and ourselves, the effect of this obedience to the Law is to diminish the idolatrous importance of properties and possessions. Possessions, like the other concrete events of our lives, are a part of the larger whole. This describes who I am in very much the same way the clothing of a friend reminds me of that person. The Law of God warns us not to tamper or interfere with such choices; they are protected by the Law within the preserved life space of the human being. It is no accident that one of the common strategies of totalitarian religions or political systems is to eliminate that preserved space.

Throughout its pages the Bible shows us a more splendid view of man and woman. God is so sure of himself that he is not threatened by our individuality. In the same way, when we welcome the intention of the eighth commandment in our relationship to the giftedness we discover in other human beings, it becomes possible for us to welcome rather than envy that giftedness.

Part of the uniqueness of human personhood is what may be described as the talents and skills that are a distinctive part of each person. This commandment sets the stage for a stewardship view of life and community. When the neighbor is honored for his or her uniqueness, and encouraged to express that giftedness within the total community, then the whole community benefits. But when envy and resentment become dominant in relationships so that the unique giftedness of each person is feared or repressed, then the community loses a profoundly important human asset.

Two Larger Questions

Here, then, is a human value that all human beings cherish if we are honest with ourselves. We are thankful for a unique signpost in the eighth commandment which shows to us God's approval of our right to ownership. This right is enforced by God as our neighbors are warned against the theft of the things we own. But we must ask two larger questions. First, if property is a human value, then in what way should we "value" things? There is also a second question—why is it that there is a certain uneasiness we feel about the possession of things?

We become uneasy in our feelings about possessions when we love them too much. If we value them too much they produce a distinct kind of nervousness.

Jesus described this difficulty for the soul in his parable about the man who filled his barns with possessions of the earth and then found, beyond the boundary of his own inevitable death, that he had no treasure in heaven. The moths had eaten away his possessions and he had nothing to show for the many years of gathering.

There is a second form of uneasiness that we feel. We know that problems of rust and decay assault every possession. Finally, even those few antique items which we were sure would gain value with age also prove no match for the thieves of time and forgotten memory.

The fact is that only righteousness and love gain value with time. For these reasons we have certain markers alongside the trail for our life journey. One signpost honors our human concreteness and the stewardship of our lives as keepers of the parts of the earth entrusted to our love. From this signpost with its stern warning to all burglars, "Thou shalt not steal," we discover that we shall have and hold parts of the earth throughout our life journey. Those possessions of ours will tell stories about us and our priorities. No society, church, or individual has the right to steal them away from us.

We need to express our concreteness through these things that we hold in our hand. We enjoy the earth and property, which is the fruit of the earth, and we steward these gifts best of all when we do not belong to them. "Seek ye first the kingdom of God and his righteousness, and all these things shall be added to you," Jesus said. Once that vital wisdom is upset and possessions become the value we treasure too greatly or love too much, then we no longer are the stewards of the possessions in our hands. Instead, we have become the slaves of those possessions. They have become the kingdom and the king.

We should feel very uneasy when that shift has happened! The answer to this danger of imbalance is not the total rejection of the earth and its treasures, because in such a lifestyle scenario we have walked away from our rightful stewardship responsibility toward material possessions. Such a response may be the correct stance for certain people as they live out their discipleship, but it cannot be the correct rejoinder for other people.

Henry David Thoreau wanted to live his life in an ideal natural environment where he was not involved with the mundane problems of employment, property, society, and money. But he nevertheless returned each weekend to his parents' home to eat their food and wash his clothes. He drank water provided by an organized municipality, and that water district was funded through taxes which were paid by citizens on the basis of property which they held and for which they were responsible.

It is impossible to walk or run away from possessions, because it is impossible to escape the earth. We need a better way. That is the way of wisdom in which our priorities are clear-headed about the possession of things. It is a kingdom perspective that sees all of life under the reign of Jesus Christ. Therefore our stewardship of the earth is one more extension of a greater value. This value holds that all of life is seen as a trust which grows out of a beloved relationship.

-11-

A Future to Invest In

One of the ways that fortunes have been made, and lost, too, is in the purchase of undervalued properties which are then rehabilitated or in some way reconstituted for resale or development. These are usually risky investments, but they are a fundamental ingredient in the art of making money with money. The big questions in this kind of investment are these—just how undervalued is the property? Is it low in value for reasons that cannot be reversed? Does the property deserve the investment?

The riskiest land purchase I have ever heard of is the one that happened more than 500 years before Christ. It is a case study in undervalued land purchase that turns out well. Jeremiah was a prophet famous both for his prophecies of judgment and also for his promises of hope.

Words of judgment make up most of the pages of his book, but right in the middle of that stern book is the narration of a remarkable and even lyrical incident; Jeremiah is instructed by God to spend his money on an investment in land and then to speak to the people dramatic words of hope on the basis of that land purchase. This incident happens just a few weeks before the city of Jerusalem is defeated in battle and destroyed by the Babylonian armies. The citizens of Jerusalem are then taken away to Babylon as prisoners of war.

Jeremiah is counseled by God to buy a field in Anathoth from his uncle. It is no surprise that his uncle Shallum is eager to sell his property since at the very moment of sale, Anathoth, which is 2 ½ miles northeast of Jerusalem, is occupied by the soldiers of Babylon. They are preparing their siege mounds for the final attack upon the city.

A Prophecy in Property

This is not undervalued property; it is worthless by any standard of investment criteria; it is a little like buying a house in the French quarter of Shanghai in December 1941. Jeremiah goes through with the purchase though he does complain to the Lord about it, which is his usual custom. Following that strange financial transaction, the Lord gives the prophet a word of prophecy to share with all the people. It becomes the very greatest message of messianic hope that Jeremiah is to speak throughout his whole career. His words will have a significance far beyond his own time and place. Indeed, Jeremiah's act becomes a lived-out sign to that people in Jerusalem in the year 586 B.C. and also to the whole human family. It reveals that God would respect and heal a broken people by his own mighty act:

> For thus says the Lord: Just as I have brought upon this people all this great calamity, so I will bring upon them all the good that I promise them. Fields shall be bought in this land of which you are saying, It is desolate, without man or beast; it is given into the hands of the Chaldeans. They shall buy fields for money, sign the deeds, seal them, and secure witnesses in the land of Benjamin, in the places about Jerusalem, in the cities of Judah, in the cities

of the hill country, in the cities of the Shephelah, and in the cities of the south; for I will restore their fortunes, says the Lord (Jeremiah 32:42–44).

As a Christian in this century, I have some questions that I try to ask myself: Where are the undervalued properties near me? How can I buy my generation's field at Anathoth? And what does it really look like to make such a purchase?

When it comes to the problems of undervalued property—they are everywhere. There are many people and groups of people who are like Anathoth because their lives are occupied by hostile forces. As a result, those who are in the business of evaluating property for investment purposes have written off the future prospects of these Anathoth people. The hostile occupation, which may be spiritual, psychological, political, or chemical, is a reality. It does not help to try to deny how devastating that occupation may be. The fact remains true that what these people need more than anything else is to be revalued both by themselves and by a few other people who believe in their future. They need to become a party to the sign of hope—the investment in their future. We who are Christians can, by the grace of God, become those "few other people." When we are, we will make a difference between the despair that discounts value and the hope that adds value—even though the proof of the true value may take time just as Jeremiah's purchase did.

The second question concerns the "how." How can I invest in an undervalued life just as Jeremiah invested in an undervalued property near Jerusalem? This brings me to the best definition I know of caring and investment in youth in the Christian church—and one Christian church in particular. Our task in youth ministry is not to rename the field, not to imagine away the problems at Anathoth, but also not to treat Anathoth as if it were too hopelessly occupied to have a valuable future. Our task is to make a long-term investment in the future of that field and to do so carefully and optimistically. We believe in this future for one reason, and that is because of the transforming grace of Jesus Christ. But that is reason enough!

What Jeremiah Didn't Know

We have so much more to go on in helping us to have the boldness to invest than did the prophet Jeremiah in 586 B.C. We know much more of the whole story than he did. Jeremiah looked forward to the future when God's righteous branch would spring forth from dry ground. But we have experienced that righteous branch, Jesus of Nazareth, and the first fruits in our own lives of the actual fulfillment of Jeremiah's hope. No wonder he complained about the task that God gave him to do!

We, however, have our own experiences of the plan of God to add value to the lives of people; that plan has been validated to us every time we see a man or a woman, young or old, experience God's love in their lives. And it is this reality that makes our task no burden but an adventure.

I am telling the truth! I have seen it for myself—I have seen young men and women who have been harmed by destructive influences and experiences, yet they have found radically new beginnings because of the power of Christ's love at work in their lives.

The one feature in Jeremiah's act of hope that we must not miss is the historically concrete nature of his act. The prophet did something concrete and definite when he purchased a highly suspect piece of land. He weighed out seventeen shekels of silver, he signed deeds with witnesses. This concreteness is profoundly important because it becomes just one more Old Testament sign of the grand concreteness that will win our salvation when "the Word became flesh and dwelt among us."

We should never give up either because of the various occupation armies or because of our own feelings that we by ourselves cannot make any difference. The people who cause hope to spring up are those who keep at it and keep on buying the fields at Anathoth. This is how the world is changed.

What is our Anathoth in the time and places where we live? It is the next generation. I am convinced that the youth in every culture are the most decisive Anathoth landscape that there is. For some youth, there are hostile occupation forces that threaten them in very concrete and destructive ways. There is no more important investment for the Jeremiahs of our century than to invest in youth at precisely the most vulnerable years of their growing up. Those are the years we describe as the junior high period, the twelve- through fifteen-year-old young person.

When most of us look back to the time of our own youth, there are two years (plus or minus) of that memory journey only dimly remembered if remembered at all. These two years fit within the seventh to ninth-grade school years, the time of early teens. I have wondered why there is this memory block, and I think I have finally found some preliminary answers.

I can think of one major reason for this protective forgetfulness. It is because these two years for most kids are not as happy as the other years of growing up. What causes this unhappiness? It is the result of two things that happen to boys and girls during this time: the one is the powerful, almost unmanageable experience of growing that takes place during the early teens. The second is the disconnectedness that each girl and boy feels and sometimes wants and always fears.

By its very nature the growth process is stressful, but never as much as during the junior high years. For one thing, everyone grows at a different rate and with different side effects. Girls are completely out of sync with their male classmates; and for much of the time in junior high, girls are physically "older" than most of the boys in their class. And their social interests have shifted sharply from the interests of boys their age. Males begin junior high peacefully as little boys, but they experience the swiftest changes of their whole lifespan in these two years (especially during the summers) as their bodies become muscular and taller and their faces more angular. This physical, emotional experience of becoming a man is an awkward time during which voices crack and feet stumble.

"A Time between Times"

The intensity of growing creates a time between times, a disconnectedness. The body he or she is growing accustomed to is disconnected from the earlier boyhood or girlhood form; and, yet, it has not settled in as a young adult body that is finally mine. It is a "time between times" physically. We should not, therefore, be surprised by the fact that many youth develop emotional feelings about self-image problems. These will continue to intimidate a young person far beyond junior high years and will sometimes last for a lifetime. These feelings of awkwardness produce in most youth a social disconnectedness that is sometimes played out by withdrawal from socially demanding situations. Especially for boys, there is often during these years a withdrawal from athletically demanding sports events. This is one reason that physical education classes which are poorly taught in junior high are so often damaging to a boy's self-confidence. It is a disconnectedness that hurts the teenager; but, nevertheless, it is adopted as a protective disconnectedness.

This time between times, is, nevertheless, one of the most significant formation periods in any person's life. During these years, academic habits are established that set the stage for later career choices. It is also the time when decisions are made about such large health questions as the use or nonuse of alcohol, drugs, tobacco; and in junior high, interpersonal relationship patterns are formed that have long-term consequences in the self-understanding of each young person. What baffles me is that adults are so unaware of the significance of these years in the lives of the next generation. As vital a time as this is in the development of a human being, why is it that so few creative and helpful strategies have been worked through in favor of youth in their early teens by the adults who know and love them?

Even if we wanted to, we cannot stop the growing. But we certainly can help out with the disconnectedness. I am not calling for tighter discipline at home, because this is the time when a teenager needs to experience increasingly greater freedom from parental supervision—not more supervision. Therefore, I'm not arguing for more control and the insidious connectedness of control. The question is: How can this connecting be enriched? I believe that there are some strategies we can follow. Here are five strategies as a starting place:

Five Strategies to Follow

First, everyone involved with teenagers needs to be realistic about what is happening. This is the right time to talk frankly about how normal the experiences of growing up really are. The questions teenagers have about male and female sexuality and the stressful interpersonal relationship between boys and girls need to be realistically talked about in a decision-making way with accurate information available. Families and their teenagers need to communicate about the values that mean the most and about how those values relate to practical questions like buying cars and clothes, about finding happiness, about such health threats as drugs, alcohol, and tobacco.

Sometimes these discussions take place at a scheduled moment but usually they happen at unplanned en route moments just because the teenager and his or her family feels safe enough to talk and listen. Sometimes this very important connecting takes place because the youth group at church takes the leadership in helping families and youth to think through the questions and meaning of the junior high years from a Christian perspective. In both places at every time when such communication can happen, the good result is that relationships are given the chance to be enriched and strengthened. This is a very important building block in the life of a teenager, because the loneliness cycle is broken in favor of relationship.

Second, I believe it is vital for parents to reach out creatively and supportively toward the friends of their teenager. This friendliness, which is always important, is especially so during the junior high years. One way to be this kind of friend to your teenager's friends is by volunteering to drive for school, scout, church, and also informal outings. I think the best rule is the total availability rule so that you can be present and helpful when needed, if at all possible.

Since these are pre-driver's license years, the opportunities are usually plentiful. The bonus we who are parents receive is the chance to get to know, in a supportive way, our children's friends and acquaintances. Since peer groups are so critically important to the junior high teenager, parents need to find ways of becoming friends with the youth who make up their teenager's circle.

Only a few parents actually do this. Therefore, when you are willing to be warmly supportive in this practical way, you provide a positive reference point for kids; you become something like an anchor on what is otherwise often a random, nonadult, teenage seascape. I'm talking about the kind of parental openness that is not snoopy but is eager to be an encouragement. This is the kind of parental presence teenagers really love. It is manifested in a home that is available as a friendly place to bring friends. It makes it possible for us to learn the names of our son's or daughter's classmates and to show genuine interest in what is happening in their lives too.

Then it is that we as a family connect not only with our youthful family member but with the peer relationships so important right now in our teenager's life.

A third strategy I have in mind has to do with atmosphere. I believe that we who are adults have it in our power to reduce some of the pressures weighing down many youth in their junior high years. I don't think a teenager should feel guilty for being stormy in a stormy time of life. A little shouting in a family is not grave insolence and should not be overinterpreted as if it were by the adults in the house. In this time of a young man or woman's life the adults need to know how to wait it out. With humor and love that does not give up, they can weather the times of a teenager's experimentation with freedom. We who are older need to believe in God's forgiveness for ourselves and for our youngsters when they fail as well.

Fourth, this is a time of passage, and we who create culture need to positively create rites of passage for our youth in this marvelous time of their lives and ours. This is where the celebration of a confirmation class can be so important when youth make their own decision to confess their faith. The family should cheer the change of voice in a boy. This is a time for warm and understanding celebration of the beginning of menstruation for a girl or the first whiskers in the boy now becoming a man. These are times for rejoicing, and a family can find the ways to celebrate the marvel of passage in a way that shows not only how normal everything is but also how good God has made us.

This is the way we move beyond embarrassment about ourselves toward an enthusiastic connectedness with ourselves and the grand design of creation. Fun, itself, is one of the best connectors there is; and in my opinion, there is more need for fun in families and church groups at this period of a person's life than at any other time. It is the time for the surprise stop for ice cream, the movies seen together, the adventure stories read aloud, the sports event, the special times of fathers and daughters, sons and mothers, sons and dads, mothers and daughters. The older sister or brother can make a junior high brother or sister feel very special with a visit to college or work. All these connecting events build self-confidence because they make us feel good about ourselves and what we are becoming.

Finally, this is the time when a teenager can really make a good friend of the Lord Jesus Christ who really loves teenagers and always has. These years are very special in the faith journey of a human being, because the junior high youth's mind is at a peak of alertness. The junior higher has the ability to think clearly about the full meaning and implications of Christian faith. This is one of the great moments of decision-making about the signposts in a person's life journey; and, therefore, this is a time for a thoughtful and content-oriented presentation of the claims and promises of Jesus Christ.

This is not the time to depreciate or underrate the mind of that young person in our youth group or our home who is growing so fast right in front of our eyes. This is a moment, as is every time, for respect and thoughtful engagement, because this is a time when the teenager in our home is as bright and quick as he or she will ever be. We shall never regret any of the hours spent in the encouragement of this key generation of people at a "time between times" because it is a very good time at that. If Jeremiah the prophet bought a field at Anathoth to become the sign of future hope, we who believe in the Lord of hope must do the same investing in the priceless Anathoth fields that ride skateboards in front of our house, these sojourners we know so well.

Remembering my friends who I loved in the
simpler times of youth will help me
be a friend.
Remembering the songs and the shows that they go with
makes new songs easier to learn.
Remembering my home as the place always for me
makes me more at home when I am away.
Remembering my name and the dreams I made
my own
gives me strength when people wonder who I am.
Remembering the love that found me before I could
remember
keeps life alive while I am remembering.

E.F.P.

Afterword

How do we remember? What is it that we remember? Are we at a point in modern history where remembering has been replaced by our fascination with the present and even our captivity to the present? If we wanted to remember where would we begin?

During the autumn of 1988 our church in Berkeley presented four evening lectures on the theme *Christian Faith and the Artistic Mandate*. Each evening lecture focused upon a different form of the Christian cultural mandate: music, drama, and literature. Our speaker on the evening in which we considered literature was the Nobel Prize winner for Literature in 1980, Czeslaw Milosz, Professor of Slavic Literature at the University of California in Berkeley. Professor Milosz entitled his lecture *The Erosion of Faith in America*. One of his sentences made an unforgettable impression upon me. He argued that men and women in Western culture have become "self referential." He explained that we live in a post-Christian era in which the old values that underpinned Western civilization are being replaced by individualized values that have their origin in the self.

This interior search for values means that we look to ourselves for the answers about meaning, we look to ourselves for guidance in making ethical choices, we look to ourselves in planning every move because we are our own goal. The result in literature is the steady parade of self-referential characters who have dominated our novels and films, characters who are usually bored and boring because a character in the story only really becomes fascinating when we discover his or her struggle with larger purposes and temptations and loves and fears.

When the character is self referential this larger landscape is lost unless he or she meets up with a really interesting person, someone who is not so tightly boundaried by the self. Professor Milosz helped me to understand the loneliness factor that is such a widespread characteristic of this high-speed generation that is ours near the end of the twentieth century. We are a sojourner generation and we always have been; but there is presently an unsureness about the markers that appear along the pathways of our journey route. The ability to accelerate, to increase the speed is usually not our problem, though many times a depressive kind of slowdown happens to us when we are not expecting it. It can happen at crossroads, or when the resources burn out, or when we feel lost and alone. But the greatest challenge we each face in such an age as ours is the challenge of finding true signposts that are not in reality the projections of our own desires—and then of remembering the signposts that we have found.

The greatest surprise we have is in the discovery that there is something even better than clear markers along the path. That is the friend who goes with us as our companion on the road. The truth is that this companion is the fulfillment of the grand vision in Solomon's Proverbs about the skill of wisdom and in the Law that Moses first passed along to the Israelites in the wilderness. Jesus Christ is the companion and he has been there all along.

In C. S. Lewis' story of the lad Shasta on his harrowing mountain pass trek there comes to Shasta a series of moments when he becomes aware of a silent companion who "breathes on a very large scale." This youth does not yet know about Aslan the golden Lion, Son of the Emperor from beyond the sea. But finally he can stand the suspense no longer and he looks into the dense mountain fog and asks the most cosmic of all questions, "Who are you?" Aslan answers, "One who has waited long for you to speak" (*The Horse and His Boy,* C. S. Lewis).

And now a new journey begins.

Bibliography

The following books are cited in the text by title and page number:

Bernhard W. Anderson, *Understanding the Old Testament* (Englewood Cliff, NJ: Prentice Hall, 1986).

Karl Barth, *Dogmatics in Outline* (New York: Harper & Row, 1959).

Allan Bloom, *The Closing of the American Mind* (New York: Simon & Schuster, 1987).

Dietrich Bonhoeffer, *Letters and Papers from Prison* (New York: Macmillan, 1972).

Pierre Teilhard de Chardin, *The Phenomenon of Man* (New York: Harper & Row, 1965).

Joy Davidman, *Smoke on the Mountain* (Philadelphia: Westminster, 1985).

C. S. Lewis, *The Screwtape Letters* (New York: Macmillan, 1961).

————, *The Horse and His Boy* (New York: Macmillan, 1970).

Martin Luther, *Commentary on the Sermon on the Mount* (Philadelphia: Lutheran Publication Society, 1892).

Earl F. Palmer, *The Intimate Gospel* (Waco, TX: Word Books, 1978).

H. H. Rowley, *From Moses to Qumran* (New York: Association Press, 1963).

Aleksander Solzhenitzyn, *From Under the Rubble* (Washington, D.C.: Regency Gateway, 1981).

The Complete Works of Tacitus (New York: Modern Library, 1941).

Gerhard von Rad, *Old Testament Theology* (New York: Harper & Row, 1962).